S. H. Craig

Dominion moulding Book

S. H. Craig

Dominion moulding Book

ISBN/EAN: 9783337210632

Printed in Europe, USA, Canada, Australia, Japan

Cover: Foto ©Andreas Hilbeck / pixelio.de

More available books at **www.hansebooks.com**

DOMINION

Moulding Book

S. H. CRAIG,

Manager of the Western Manufacturing Company, of London, Ont.

CONTAINING SECTIONS (FULL SIZE), OF

Mouldings, Architraves

PEW AND STAIR RAILINGS,

BRACKETS, PICKETS, LATTICE,

Scroll Work, Pallusters,

NEWEL POSTS,

INSIDE DOORS FOLDING & SLIDING DOORS

STORE DOORS,

Wood Mantles, Working Plans, &c.

LONDON; ONT.

1878.

BILL OF ITEMS.

FRAMING TIMBER, JOISTS, RAFTERS, BRIDGING, ETC.

2 sills, 4 by 10 in., 39 ft. 4 in. long.
4 sills, 4 by 10 in., 31 ft. 8 in. long.
8 posts, 4 by 6 in., 21 ft. long.
2 plates, 4 by 6 in., 39 ft. 4 in. long.
4 plates, 4 by 6 in., 33 ft. 6 in. long.
1 girder, 4 by 6 in., 39 ft. 4 in. long.
14 joists, 3 by 10 in., 16 ft. long.
103 joists, 1½ by 10 in., 16 ft. long. } First and second floors.
10 joists, 1 by 10 in., 16 ft. long. }
54 joists, 1½ by 10 in., 17 ft. long. Third floor.
10 purlins, 3 by 4 in., 16 ft. long.
42 rafters, 1½ by 5 in., 19 ft. long.
150 studs, 2 by 4 in., 21 ft. long.
112 studs, 2 by 4 in., 10 ft. long.
100 ft. braces, 2¾ by 4 in.
12 pieces, 1 by 4 in., 16 ft. long, to cut in studs to receive joists.
80 ft. raising plate, 1 by 8 in.
600 ft. bridging, 1 by 2½ in.

WEATHER BOARDS, SHINGLES, CORNICE, FLOORING, AND M FACTURED WORK.

4500 ft. weather boards, white pine, 2d common dressed.
1800 ft. sheathing and scaffolding, 1 in. pine, 3d common.
15000 shingles, pine No. 1, 16 in. long.
96 ft. lineal cornice planceer, dressed, ⅞ by 10 in.
96 ft. lineal cornice drop fascia, dressed, ⅞ by 6¼ in.
96 ft. lineal cornice crown moulding.
80 ft. lineal barge board, dressed, ⅞ by 5 in.
90 ft. lineal corner strip, dressed, 1⅜ by 4 in.
20 brackets, 9¾ in. projection, 12 in. high, 1¾ thick. (see brackets.)
96 ft. bed mould,
80 ft. stop, to form gutter on roof, 1¾ by 3 in.
3600 ft. flooring, white pine, 2d common, dressed one side, tongued and groove
500 ft. pine boards, dressed, ⅞ in., for shelving, grounds, etc.
672 ft. lineal beveled base.
48 ft. lineal plinth, 1¼ and 1⅜ rebated for base, and moulded.
912 ft. lineal band moulding,
90 ft. lineal window sill, ⅞ by 2¾ in.
90 ft. lineal window facia, ⅞ by 4 in.
80 ft. lineal carpet sill, ½ by 3½ in., beveled.
1 side light and impost door frame, with door side light and transom; frame
by 8 ft. 3 in., jambs, 6¼ wide, door posts, 3¾ in. thick; panel door, 3 by
raised and beveled, 1⅜ thick; side lights, panel below, raised and beveled
transom all glazed.
1 impost door frame, with door and transom; frame, 2 ft. 10 in. by 8 ft. 1
jambs, 6¼ wide; door, 2 ft. 10 in. by 6 ft. 10 in., raised and beveled. 1⅜
transom glazed.
16 partition door frames, 2 ft. 10 in. by 6 ft. 10 in., jambs, 5¾ in. wide, rel
1⅜ in.
2 partition door frames, 2 ft. 3 in. by 6 ft. 10 in., jambs, 5¾ in., rebated 1⅜ i
16 doors, 2 ft. 10 in. by 6 ft. 10 in., flat and beveled 1⅜ in.

2 doors 2 ft. 3 in. by 6 ft. 10 in., flat and beveled 1⅜ in.
8 cellar window frames 10 by 12 in., 3 lights.
2 common window frames 12 by 16 in., 12 lights 1⅜ in.
6   "   "   "   10 by 16 in., 12 lights 1⅜ in.
3   "   "   "   12 by 14 in., 12 lights 1⅜ in.
7   "   "   "   10 by 14 in., 12 lights 1⅜ in.
2   "   "   "   10 by 12 in., 12 lights 1⅜ in.
2 pair sash 12 by 16 in., 12 lights, primed and glazed, 1⅜ in.
6   "   10 by 16 in., 12 lights, primed and glazed, 1⅜ in.
3   "   12 by 14 in., 12 lights, primed and glazed, 1⅜ in.
7   "   10 by 14 in., 12 lights, primed and glazed, 1⅜ in.
2   "   10 by 12 in., 12 lights, primed and glazed, 1⅜ in.
8 sash 10 by 12 in., 3 lights, primed and glazed, 1 in.
2 pair venetian shutters 12 by 16 in., 12 lights, 1⅜ in.
6   "   "   10 by 16 in., 12 lights, 1⅜ in.
3   "   "   12 by 14 in., 12 lights, 1⅜ in.
7   "   "   10 by 14 in., 12 lights, 1⅜ in.
2   "   "   10 by 12 in., 12 lights, 1⅜ in.
8 mantels, plain pilaster, 4 ft. high, 5 ft. 2 in. breast.
2 flight of box stairs, as plan, carriages gained and beveled, steps and risers prepared.
1 flight of stairs to cellar, carriages and step undressed.
1 scuttle door and frame in roof 22 in. wide 3 ft. long.
Out side steps, and platform in front, as plan.
S. H. Craig's Book of Moldings contains a great variety of cornice, mouldings, base or washboard, architraves, stairs, rails, newels, balusters, brackets, mantles, doors, windows, columns, veranda posts, etc.

Remember the first thing when about to build or alter is to obtain a good plan, bill of items, and specifications. By so doing you invite competition, as each branch is brought within the comprehension of ordinary mechanics, enabling them to estimate, in a short time, intelligently. Starting thus with a definite plan, you ascertain the whole cost before commencing, and avoid alterations and disputes.

1

No. 1

No. 2

No. 3

No. 4

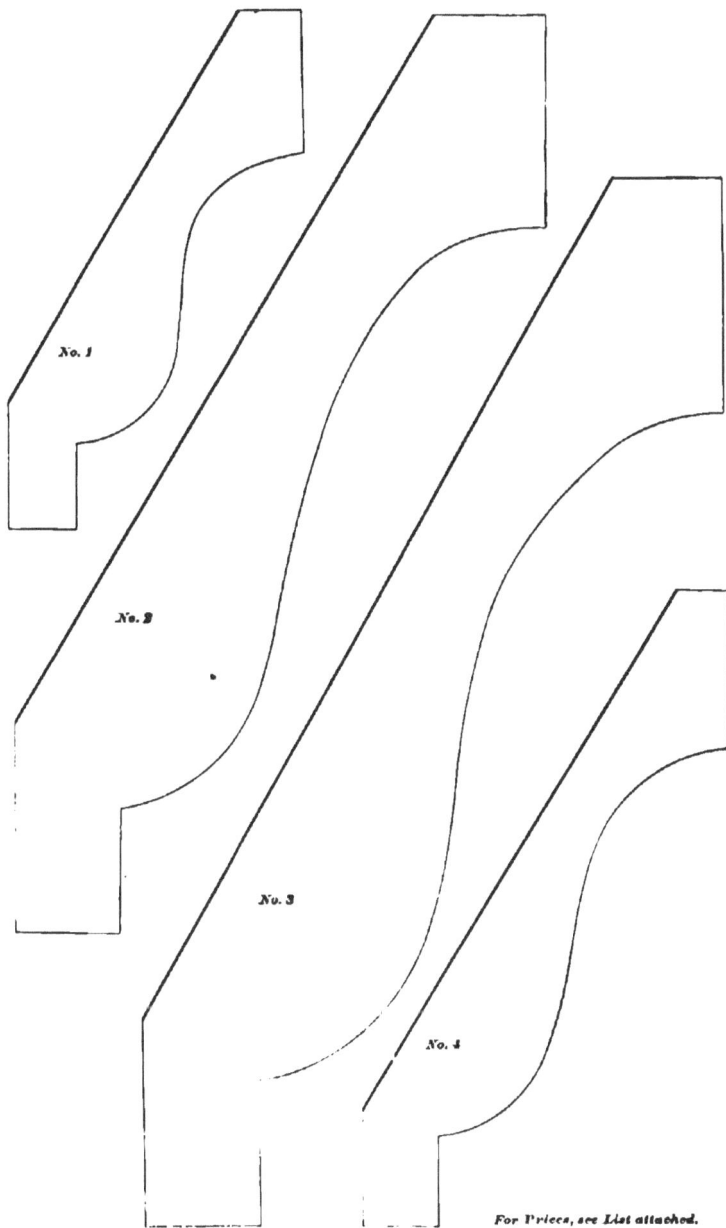

For Prices, see List attached.

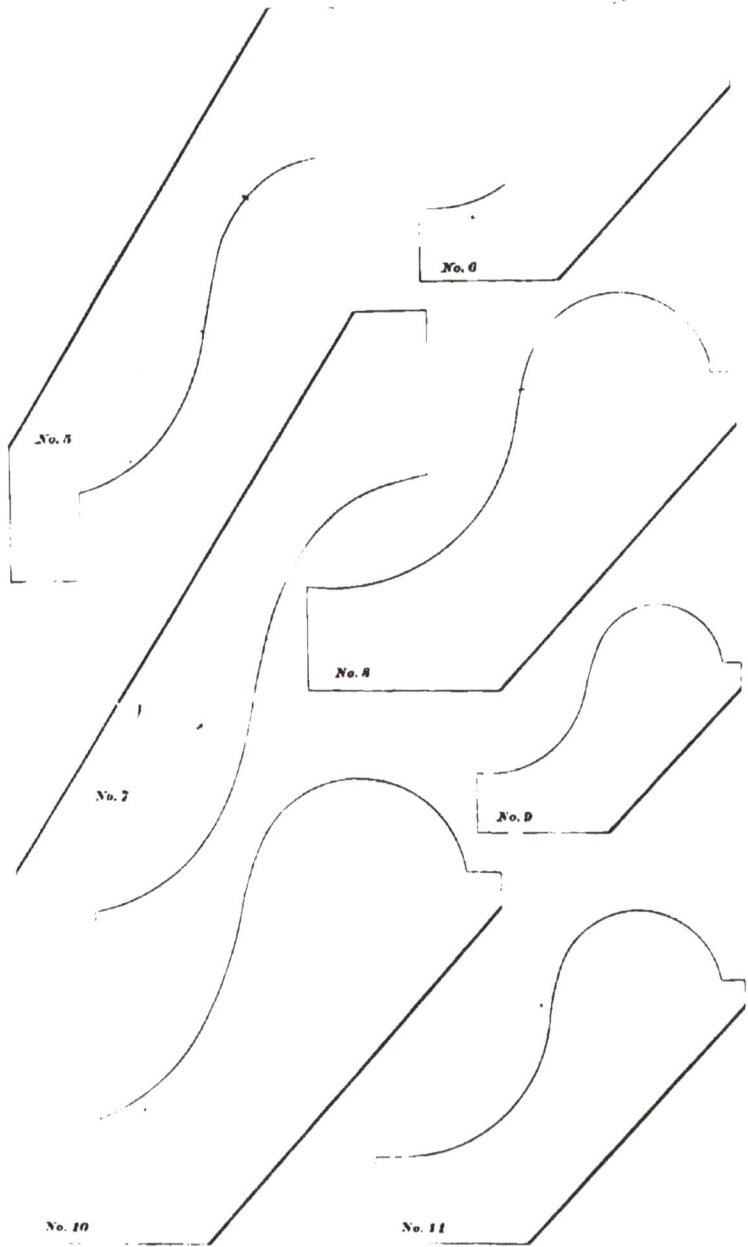

No. 5

No. 6

No. 7

No. 8

No. 9

No. 10

No. 11

No. 12

No. 13

No. 14

No. 16

No. 15

No. 17

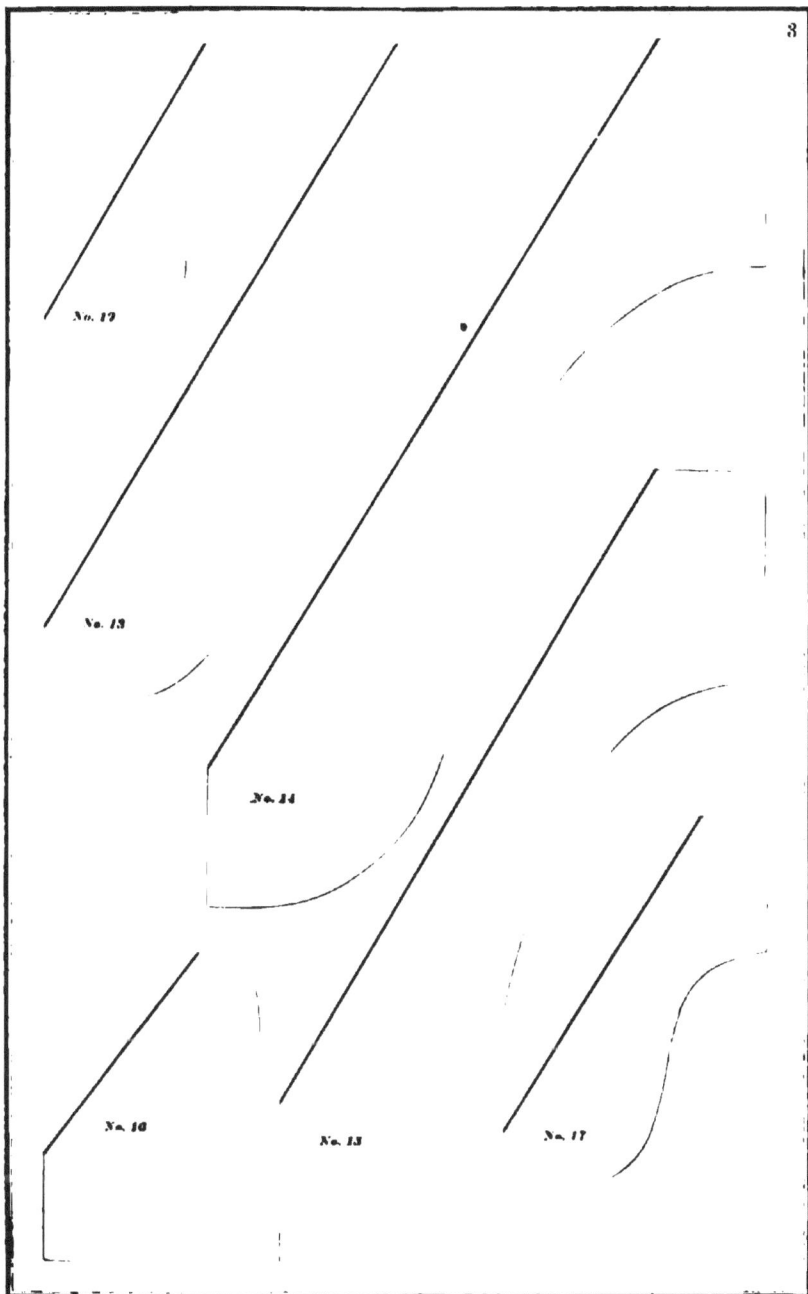

4

No. 18

No. 19

No. 20

No. 21

No. 22

No. 23

No. 24

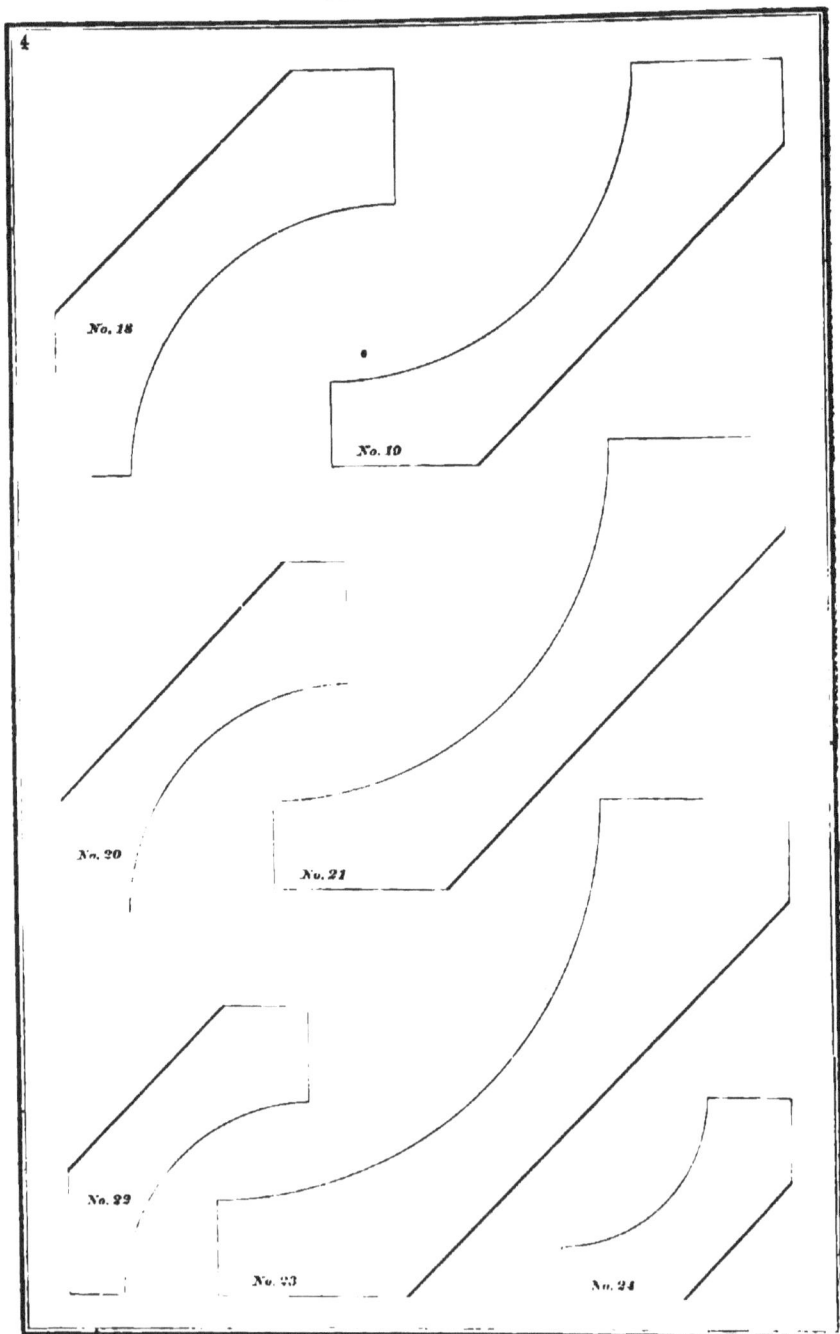

No. 25

No. 26

No. 27

No. 28

No. 29

No. 30

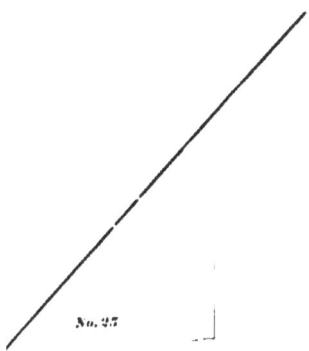

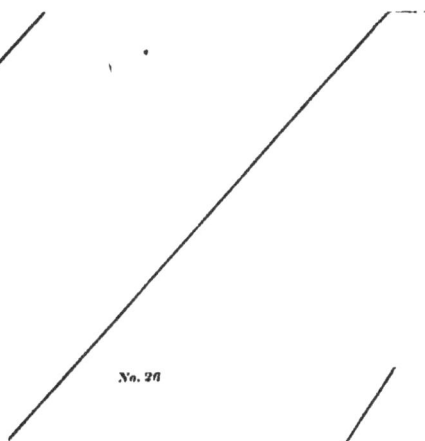

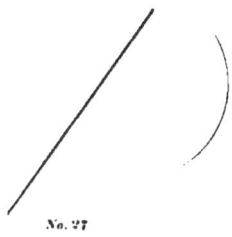

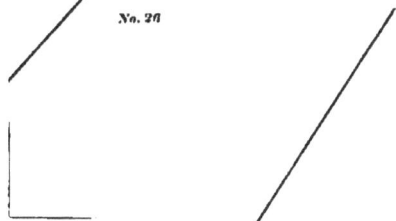

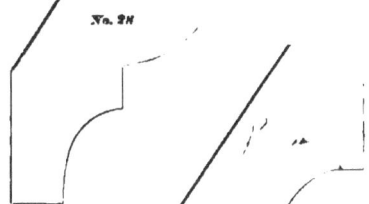

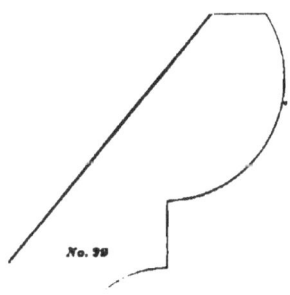

W. D. McGLOGHLON'S is the only place in the west where you can see a first-class stock to select from.

6

No. 32

No. 31

No. 33

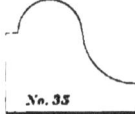

No. 35

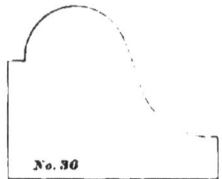

No. 36

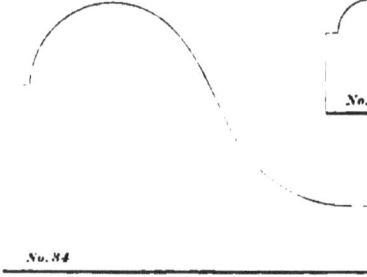

No. 34

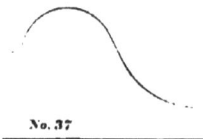

No. 37

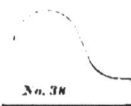

No. 38

No. 39

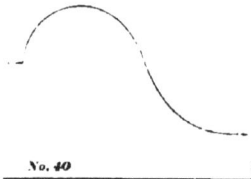

No. 40

No. 41

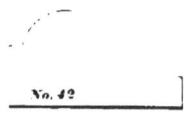

No. 42

No. 44

No. 43

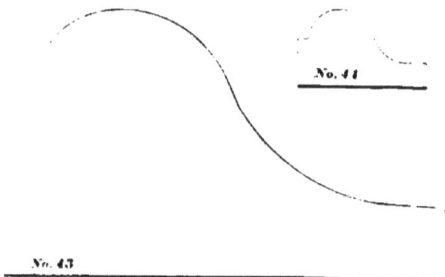

No. 45

No. 46

MOULDINGS.

 No. 47

 No. 52

 No. 58

 No. 48

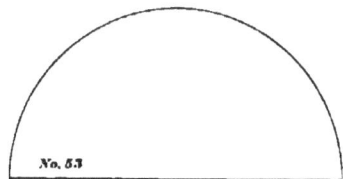 No. 53

 No. 59

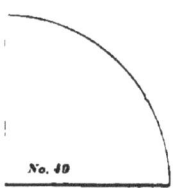 No. 49

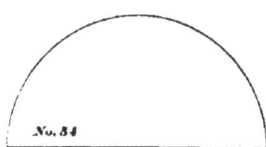 No. 54

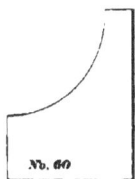 No. 60

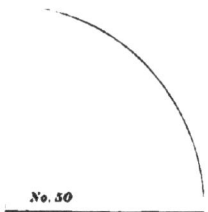 No. 50

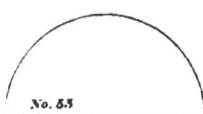 No. 55

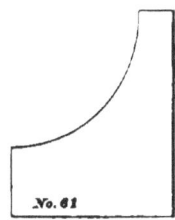 No. 61

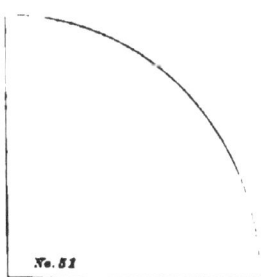 No. 51

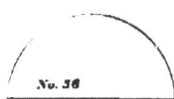 No. 56

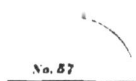 No. 57

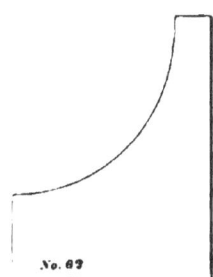 No. 62

The Fairchild Gold Pens took First Prizes and Gold Medals, at Paris and

8

Batten

No. 63

Batten

No. 64

Batten

No. 65

Batten

No. 66

Batten

No. 67

Batten

No. 68

Batten

No. 69

Batten

No. 70

No. 71

No. 72

No. 73

No. 74

No. 75

No. 76

No. 77

No. 78

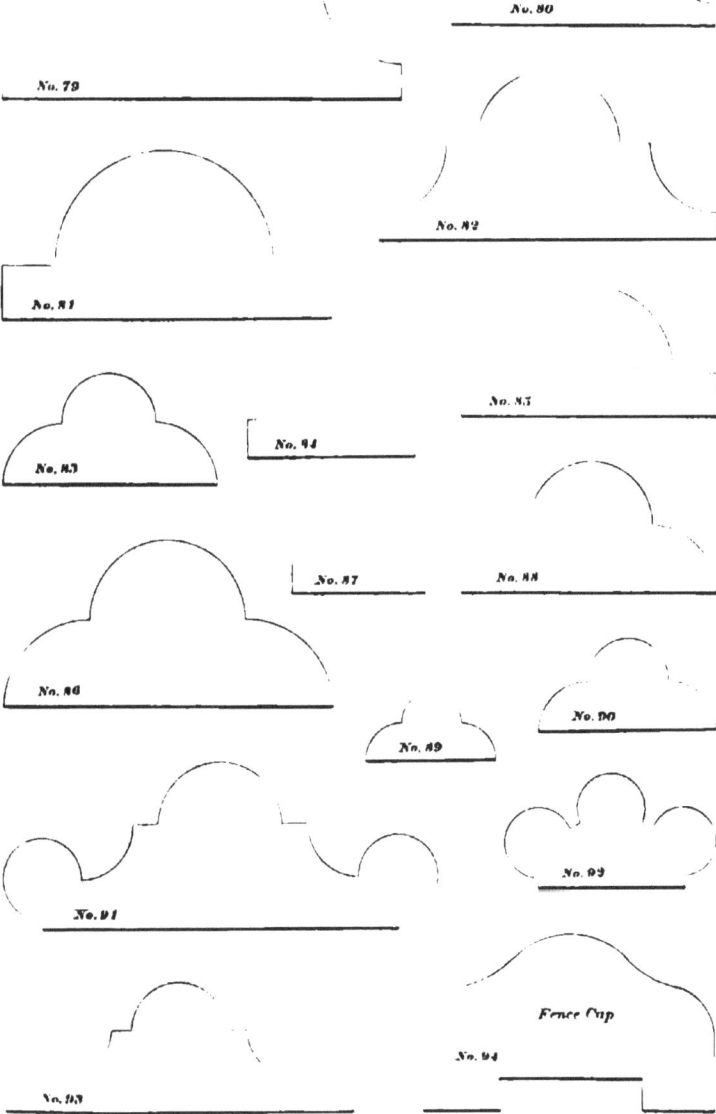

No. 80
No. 79
No. 82
No. 81
No. 83
No. 84
No. 85
No. 86
No. 87
No. 88
No. 89
No. 90
No. 91
No. 92
No. 93
No. 94
Fence Cap

10

No. 95   No. 96   No. 97

O. G. Stops, furnished any width desired.

No. 98   No. 99

No. 100   No. 101   No. 102

Stop-beads, furnished any width desired.

No. 103   No. 104

Pine or Walnut

No. 105

Thresholds for inside doors.

Pine or Walnut

No. 106

No. 107   No. 108   No. 109

No. 110   No. 111   No. 112

No. 113   No. 114

No. 115

No. 116

No. 117

No. 118

No. 119

No. 120

No. 121

No. 122

No. 123

Casings, furnished any width desired.

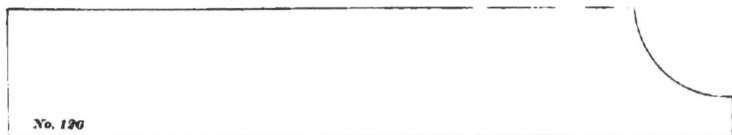

No. 124

No. 125

No. 126

12

No. 128

No. 127

No. 129

No. 130

No. 131

No. 132

No. 133

No. 134

No. 135

No. 136

No. 137

No. 138

No. 139

No. 140

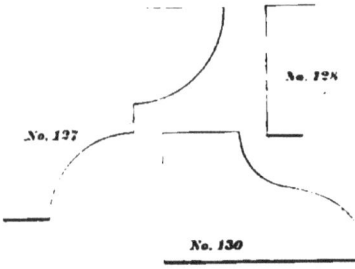

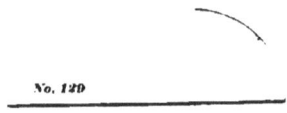

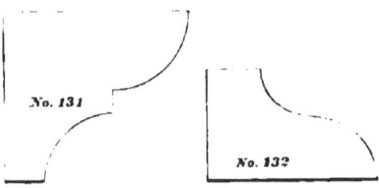

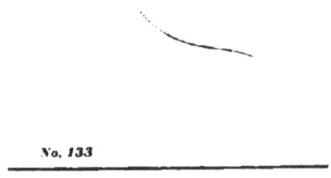

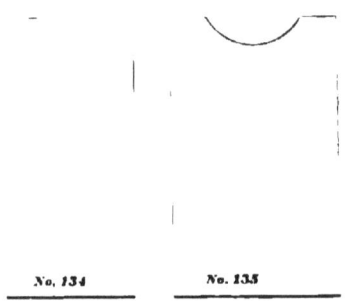

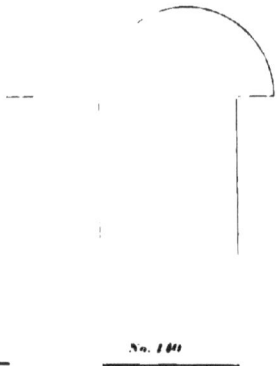

No. 141

No. 142

No. 143

No. 144

No. 145

No. 146

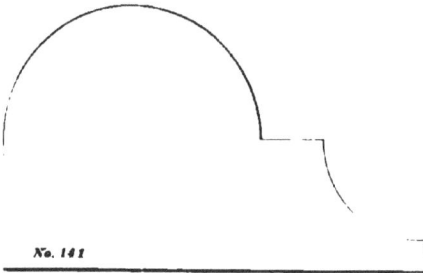

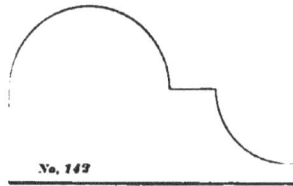

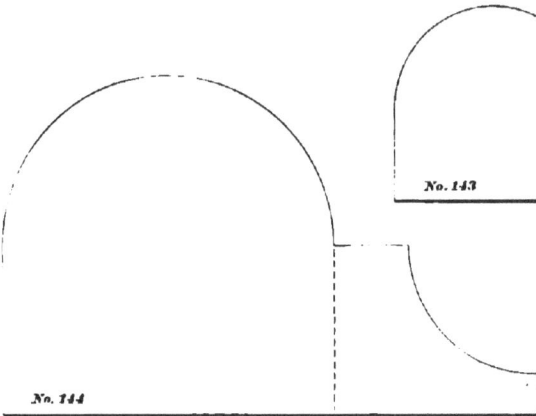

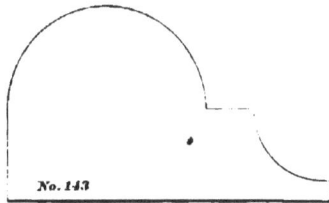

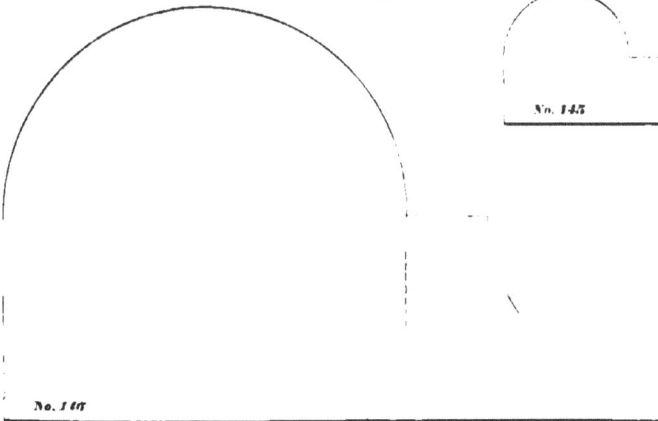

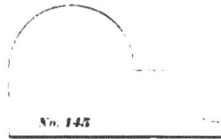

14

No. 147

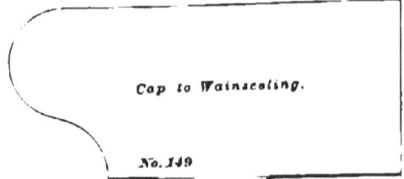

Cap to Wainscoting.

No. 149

No. 150

Partition Shoe

No. 148

No. 154

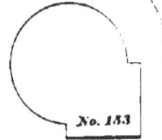

No. 153

No. 155

No. 152

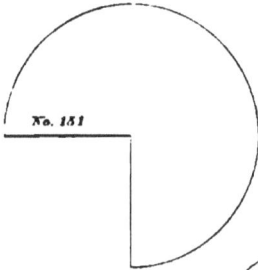

No. 151

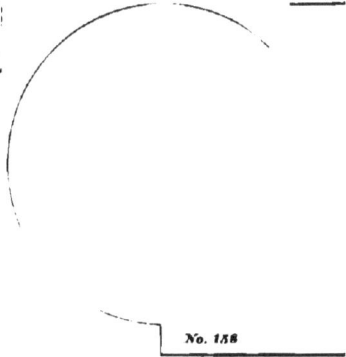

No. 156

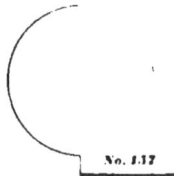

No. 137

No. 136

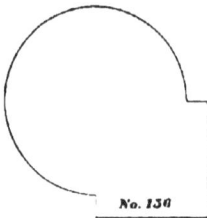

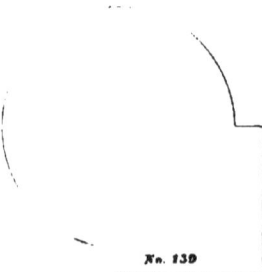

No. 139

No. 160

No. 162

No. 161

No. 163

No. 164

No. 166

No. 165

No. 167

No. 168

No. 169

No. 170

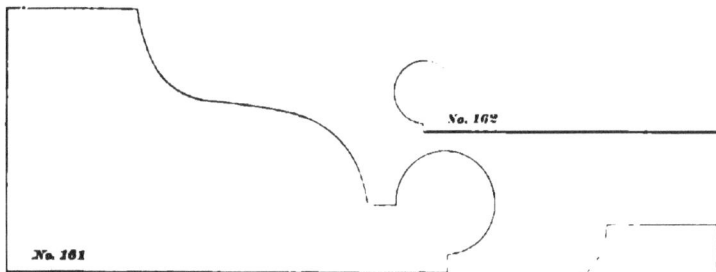

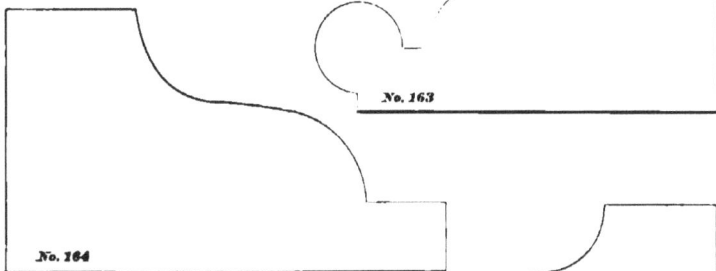

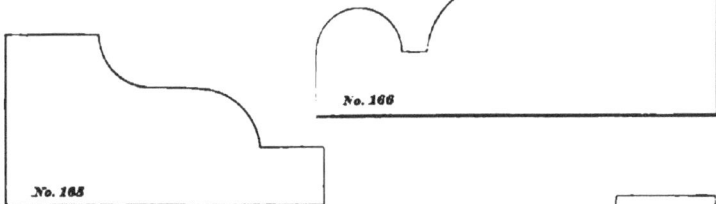

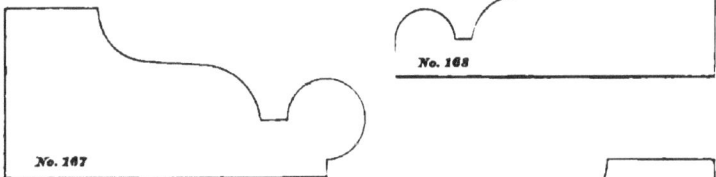

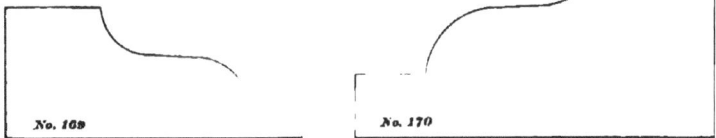

The Fairchild Gold Pens took First Prizes and Gold Medals, at Paris and Vienna World's Fairs.

16

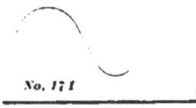

No. 171

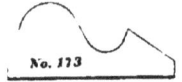

No. 173

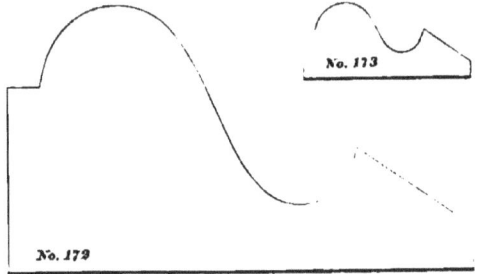

No. 172

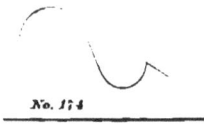

No. 174

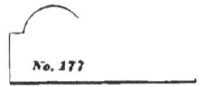

No. 177

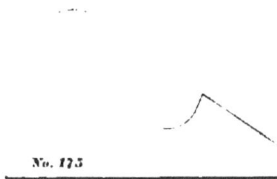

No. 175

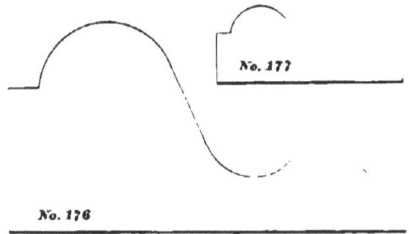

No. 176

No. 179

No. 178

No. 180

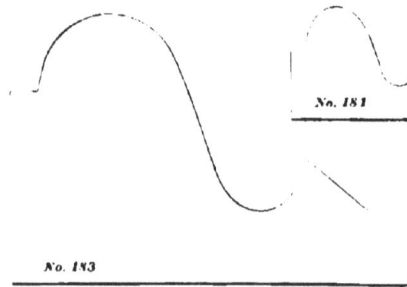

No. 181

No. 182

No. 183

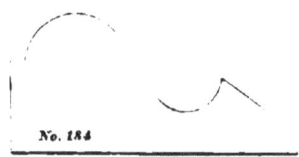

No. 184

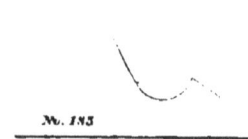

No. 185

No. 186

No. 187

No. 188

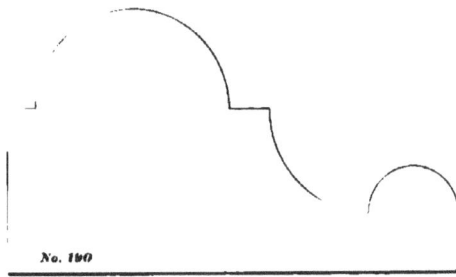

No. 189

No. 190

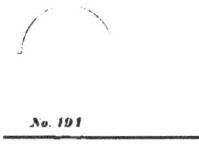

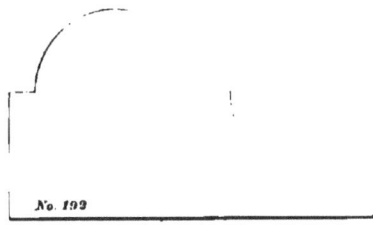

No. 191

No. 192

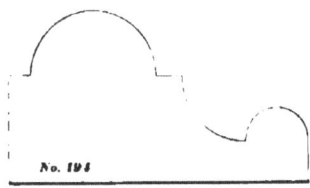

No. 193

No. 194

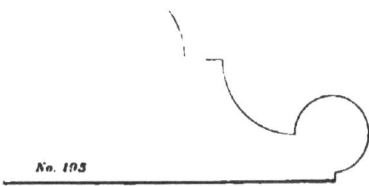

No. 195

No. 196

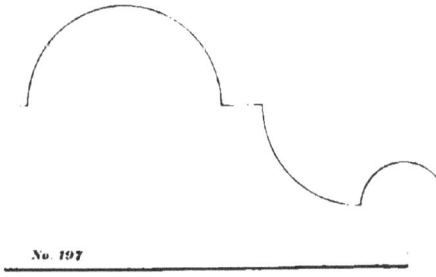

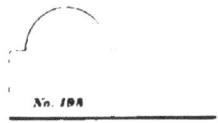

No. 198

No. 197

No. 199

18

No. 200

No. 201

No. 202

No. 203

No. 204

No. 205

No. 206

No. 207

No. 208

No. 210

No. 209

No. 211

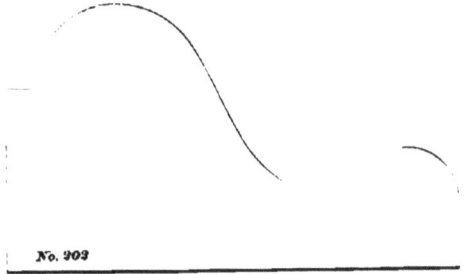

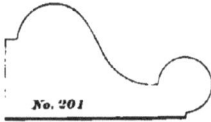

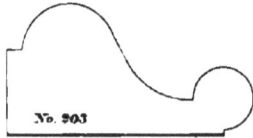

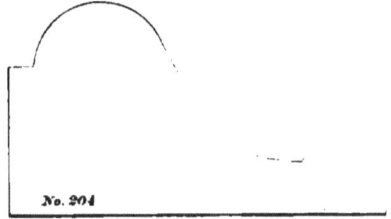

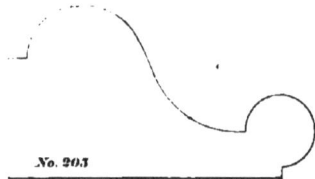

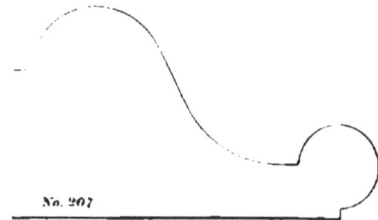

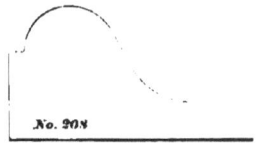

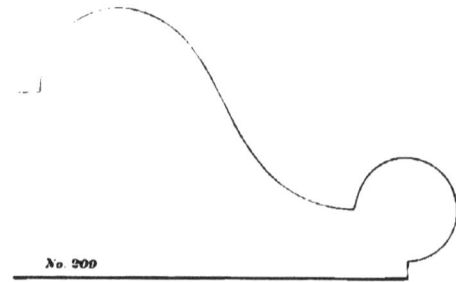

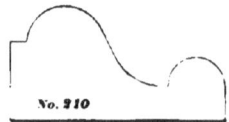

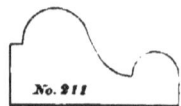

MOULDINGS.

No. 213

No. 214

No. 212

No. 215

No. 217

No. 216

No. 219

No. 218

No. 220

No. 221

No. 222

No. 223

No. 223

No. 224

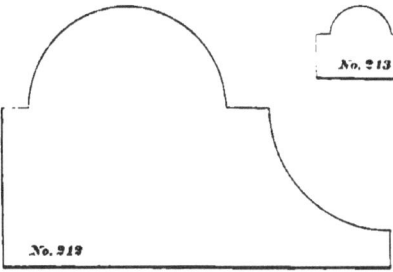

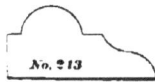

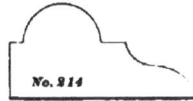

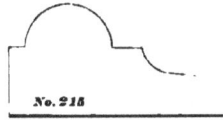

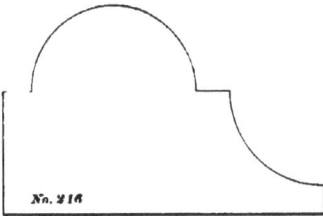

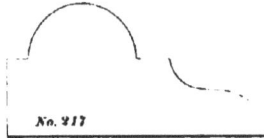

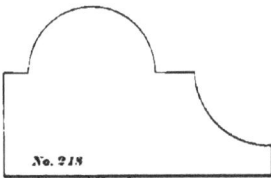

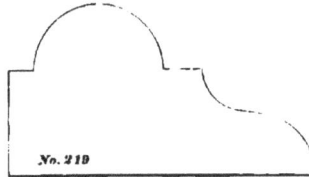

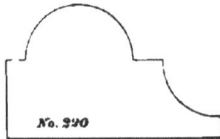

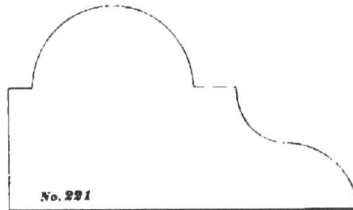

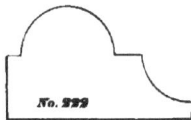

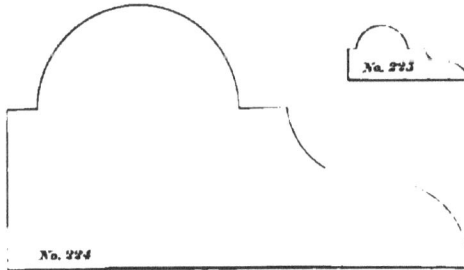

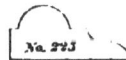

Gentlemen who have tried the W. D. McGLOCHLON Watch will have no other.

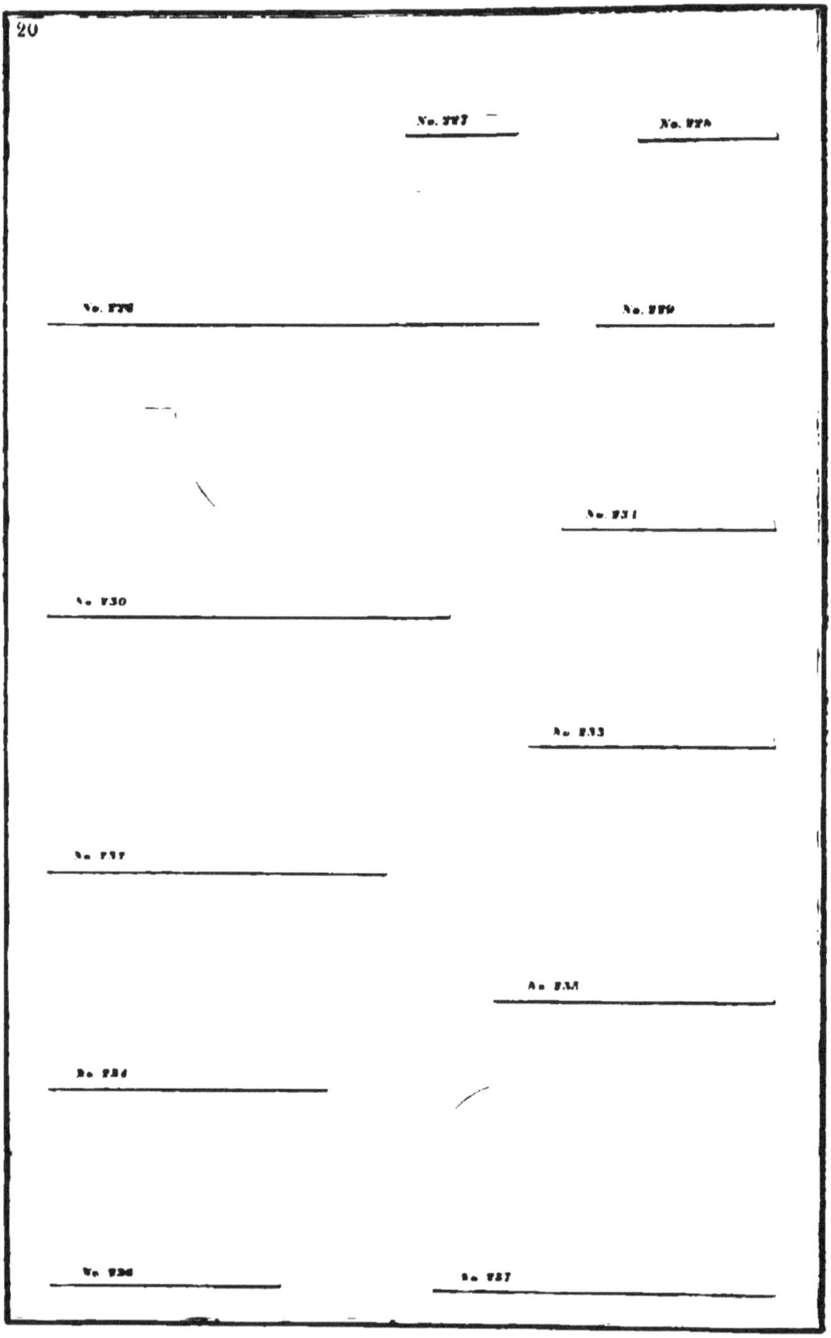

20

No. 727

No. 728

No. 729

No. 729

No. 731

No. 730

No. 733

No. 737

No. 735

No. 734

No. 736

No. 737

No. 238

No. 239

No. 240

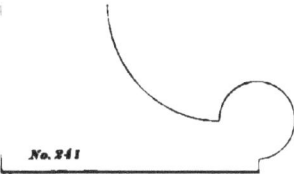

No. 241

No. 242

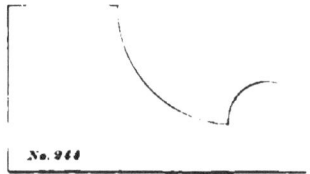

No. 244

No. 243

No. 246

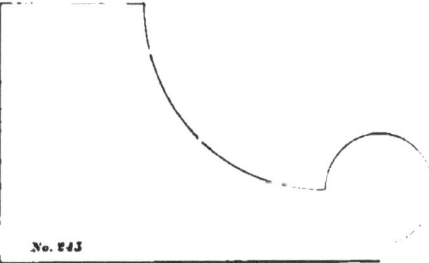

No. 245

No. 247

No. 248

No. 249

No. 250

No. 252

No. 251

No. 253

No. 254

No. 255

No. 256

No. 257

No. 258

No. 259

No. 260

No. 261

No. 262

No. 263

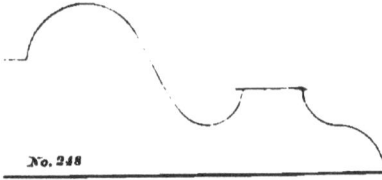

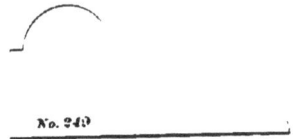

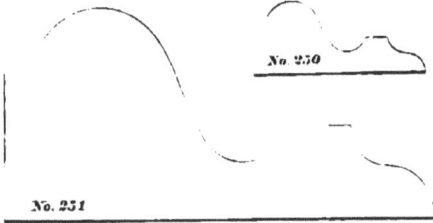

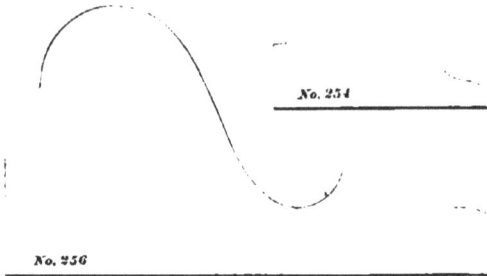

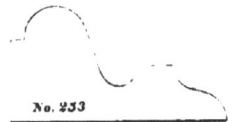

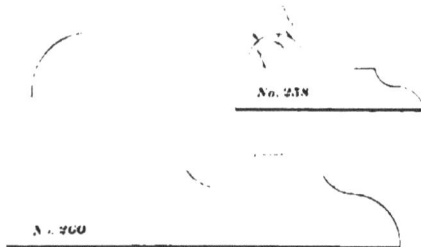

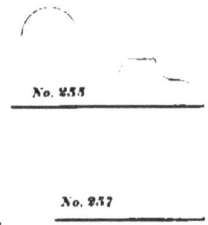

MOULDINGS.

No. 264

No. 265

No. 266

No. 267

No. 268

No. 269

No. 270

No. 271

No. 272

No. 273

No. 274

No. 275

No. 276

No. 277

No. 278

No. 279

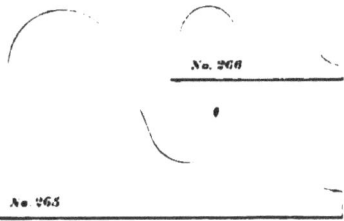

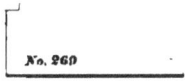

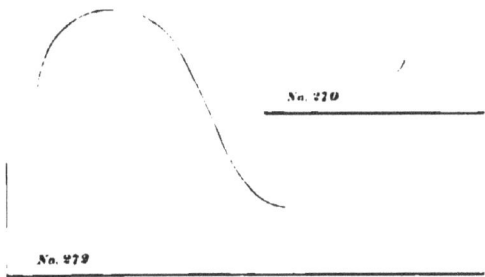

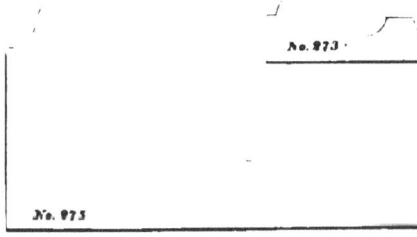

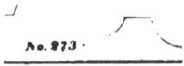

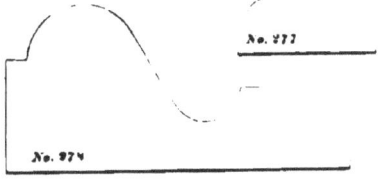

Gentlemen who have tried the W. D. McGLOCHLON Watch will have no other.

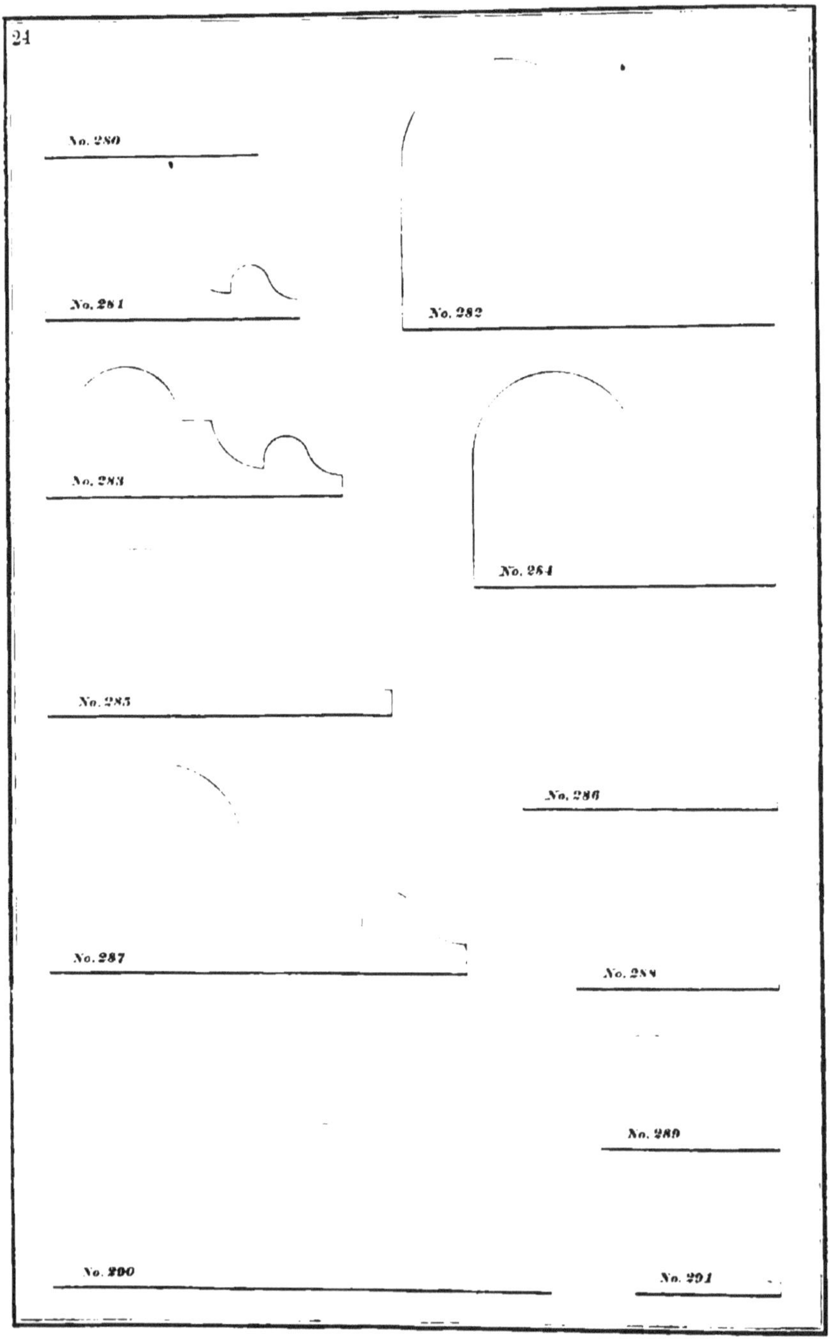

24

No. 280

No. 281

No. 282

No. 283

No. 284

No. 285

No. 286

No. 287

No. 288

No. 289

No. 290

No. 291

No. 292

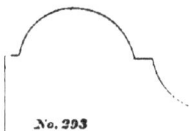

No. 293

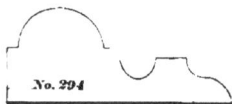

No. 294

No. 296

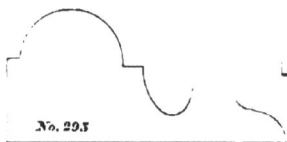

No. 295

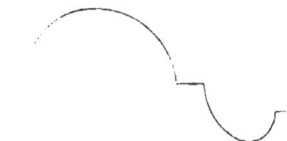

No. 297

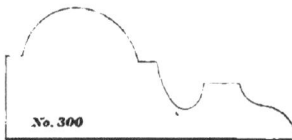

No. 298

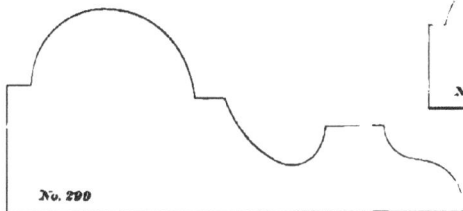

No. 299

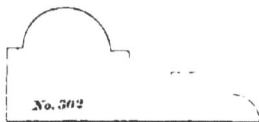

No. 300

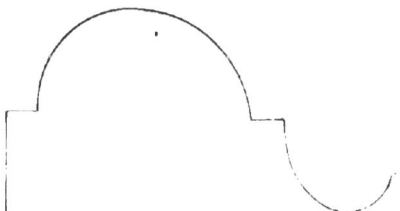

No. 301

No. 302

MOULDINGS.

26

No. 303

No. 304

No. 305

No. 306

No. 307

No. 308

No. 309

No. 310

No. 311

No. 312

No. 313

No. 314

No. 315

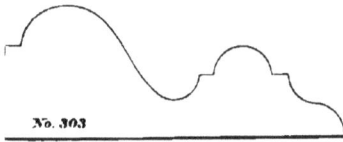

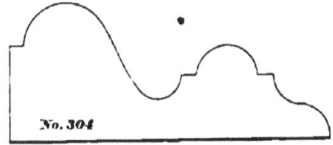

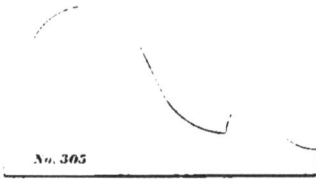

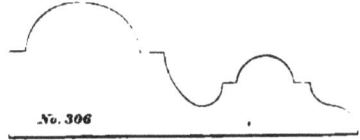

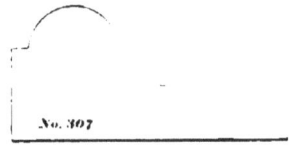

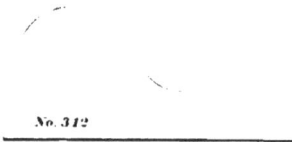

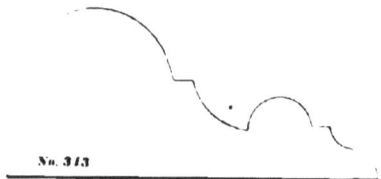

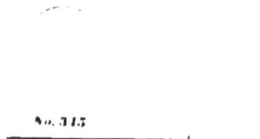

The W. D. McGLOGHLON Watch is the cheapest and best Watch in the market.

MOULDINGS.

No. 316

No. 317

No. 318

No. 319

No. 320

No. 321

No. 322

No. 323

No. 324

No. 325

No. 326

No. 327

No. 328

No. 329

No. 330

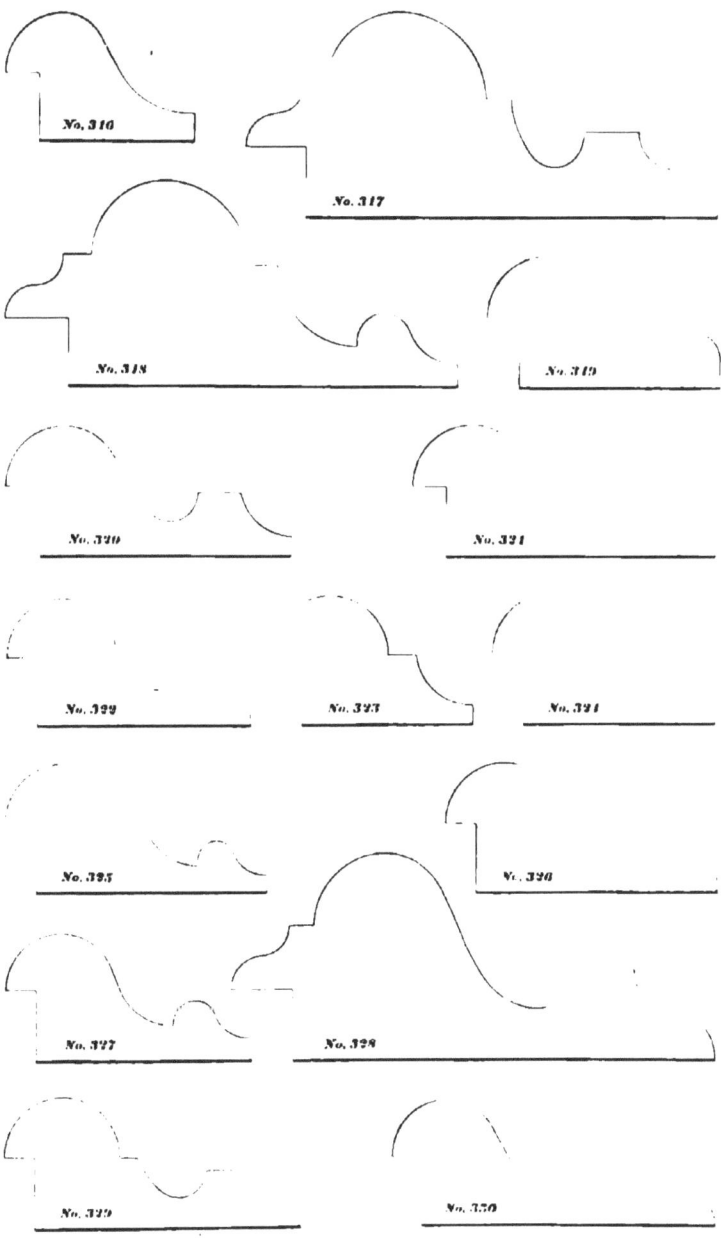

Inspect W. D. McGLOGHLON'S nice goods, before purchasing, you are sure
to be pleased in price and quality.

28

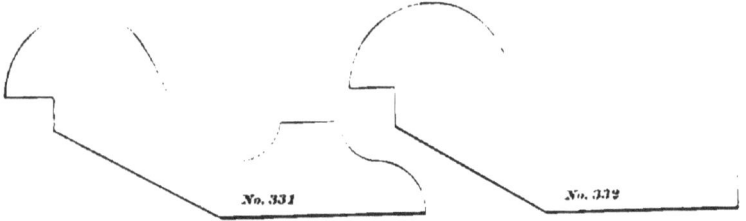

No. 331   No. 332

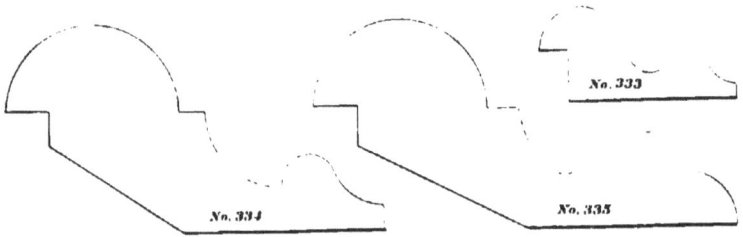

No. 333

No. 334   No. 335

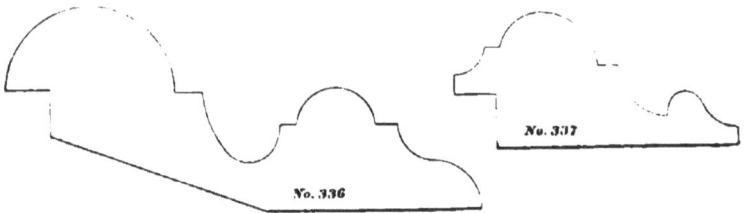

No. 337

No. 336

No. 339

No. 338

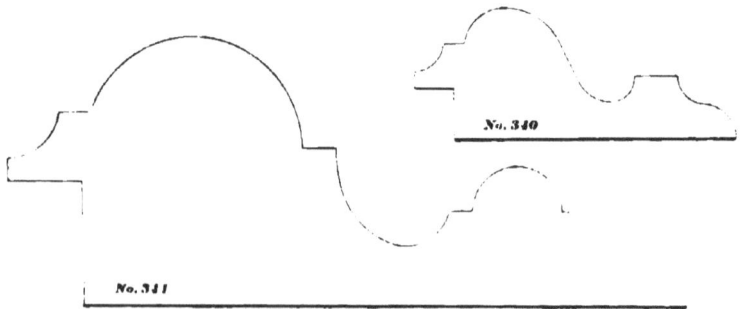

No. 340

No. 341

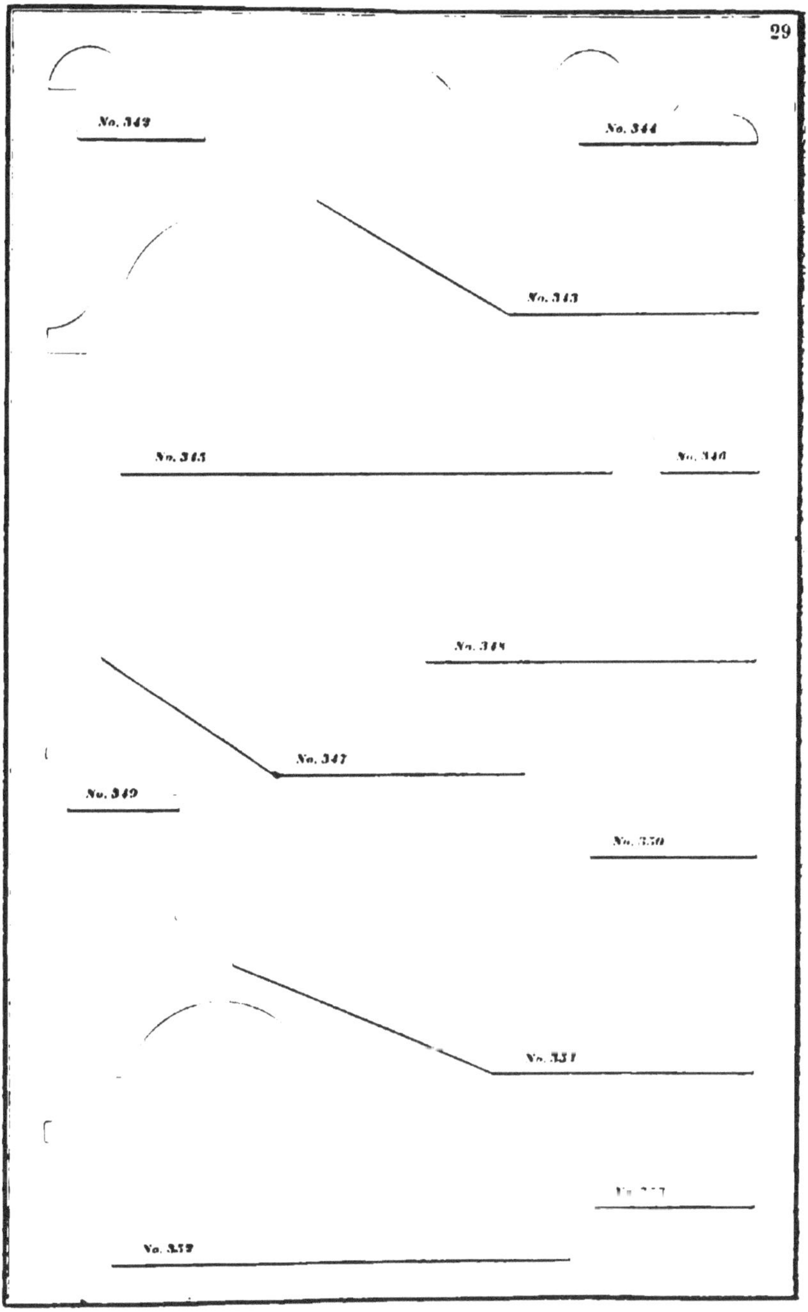

No. 342

No. 344

No. 343

No. 345

No. 346

No. 348

No. 347

No. 349

No. 350

No. 351

No. 352

No. 353

30

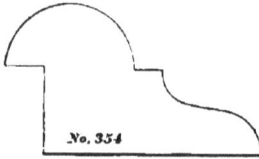

No. 354

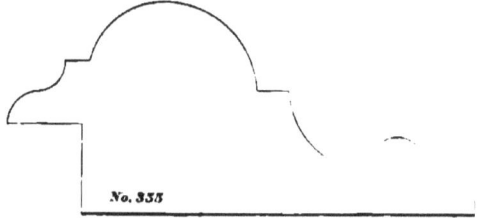

No. 355

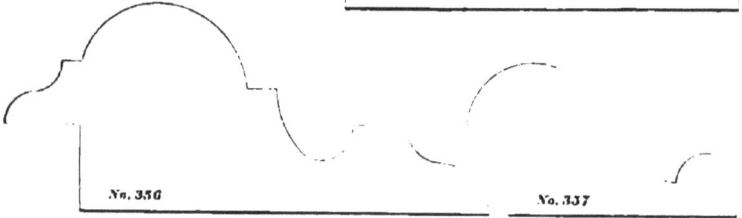

No. 356

No. 357

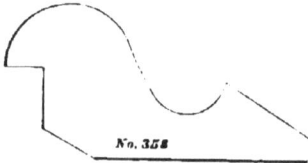

No. 358

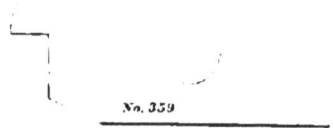

No. 359

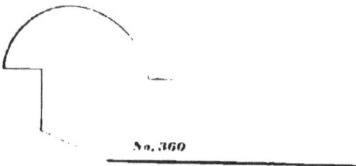

No. 360

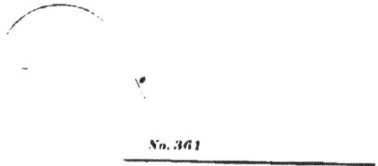

No. 361

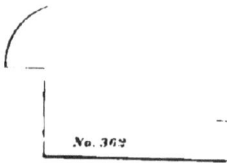

No. 362

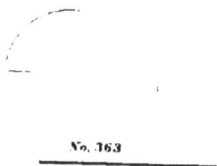

No. 363

No. 364

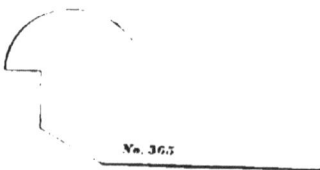

No. 365

No. 366

MOULDINGS.

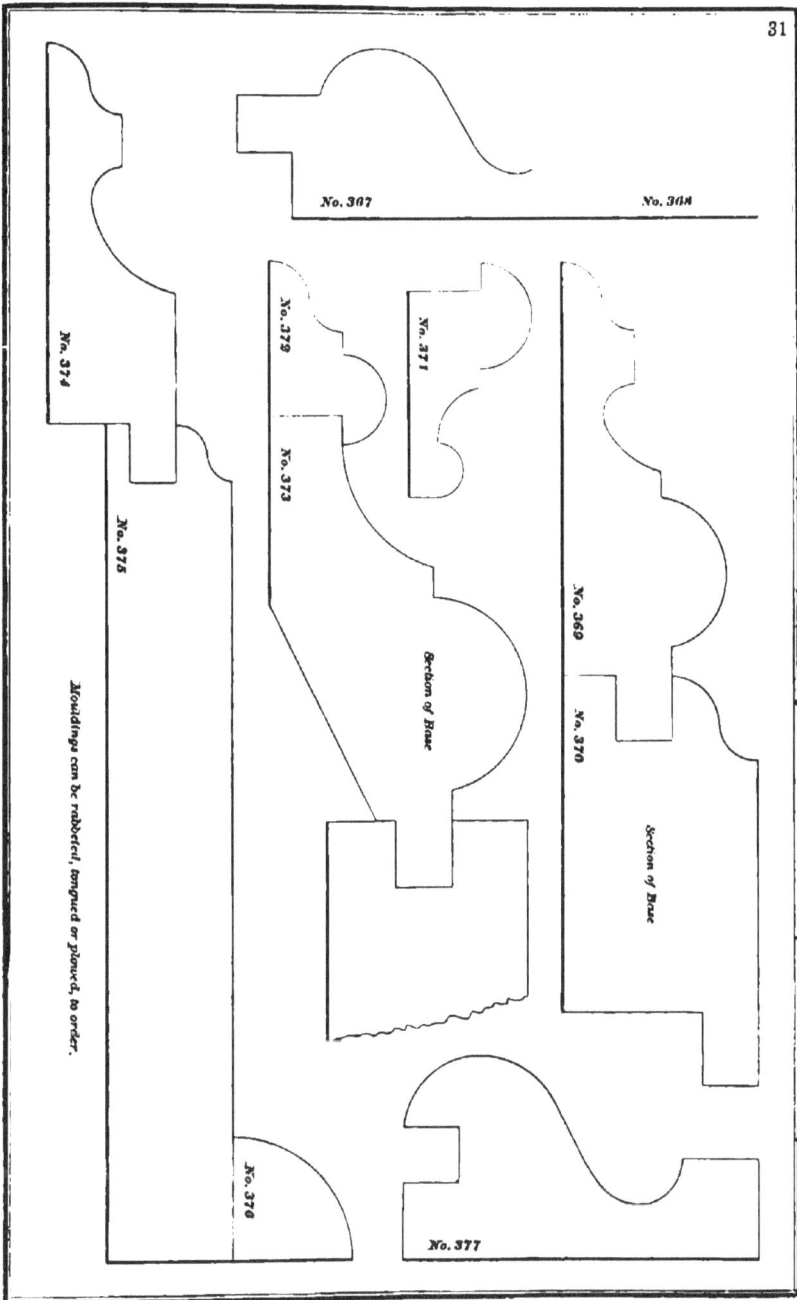

No. 367   No. 364
No. 374
No. 372
No. 371
No. 373
No. 375
No. 369
No. 370
Section of Base
Section of Base
Mouldings can be rabetted, tongued or plowed, to order.
No. 376
No. 377

You will always find W. D McGLOGHLON'S goods just as they are represented   The only first-class place in the city.

32

No. 378

No. 379

No. 380

No. 381

No. 382

No. 384

No. 383

No. 385

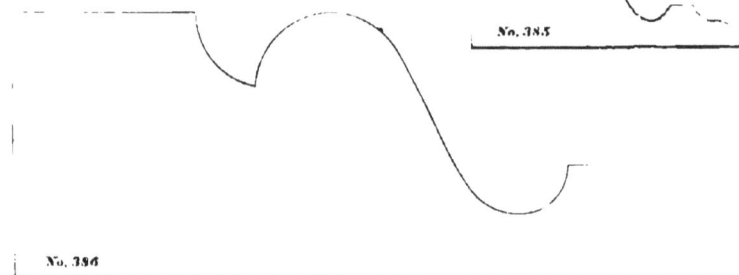

No. 386

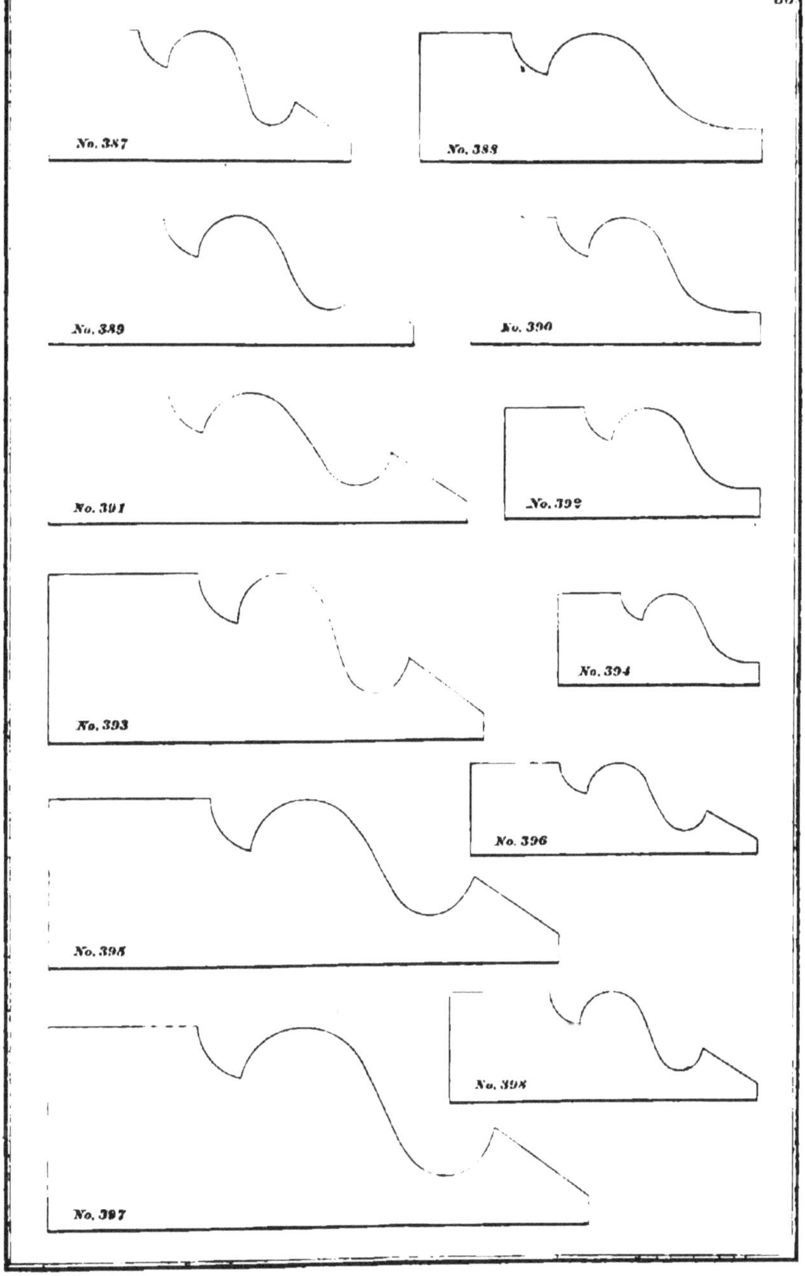

No. 387

No. 388

No. 389

No. 390

No. 391

No. 392

No. 393

No. 394

No. 395

No. 396

No. 397

No. 398

44

No. 399

No. 400

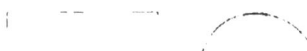

No. 401

No. 407

No. 408

No. 402

No. 403

No. 404

No. 409

No. 405

MOULDINGS.

No. 409

No. 410

No. 411

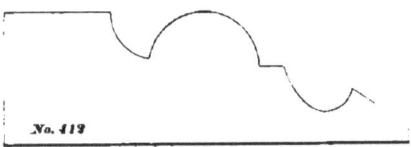

No. 412

No. 413

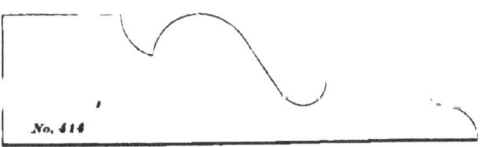

No. 414

No. 415

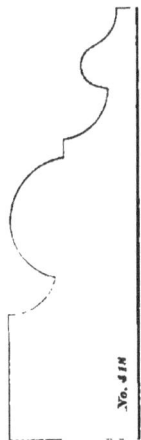

No. 418

No. 417

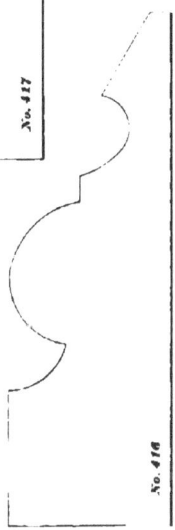

No. 416

36

No. 419

No. 420

No. 421

No. 422

No. 423

No. 424

No. 427

No. 428

No. 425

No. 426

No. 435

No. 436

No. 430

No. 434

No. 431

No. 433

No. 429

No. 432

Window Stool furnished any width and thickness desired.

Window Stool

No. 437

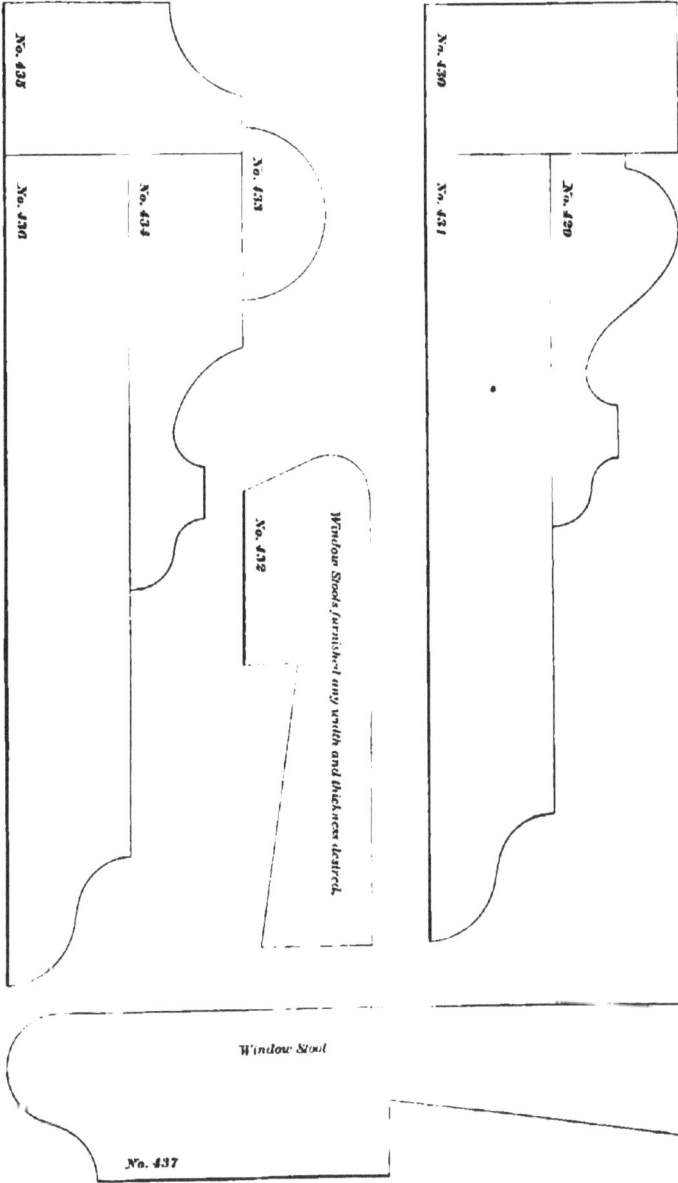

W. D. McGLOGHLON'S is the only place in the west where you can see a
first-class stock to select from.

Architraves furnished, any design desired.

No. 440

No. 439

No. 441

No. 438

No. 443

No. 442

No. 445

No. 444

ARCHITRAVES.

Architrave finish made of Walnut, Cherry, Ash or Oak to order.

40

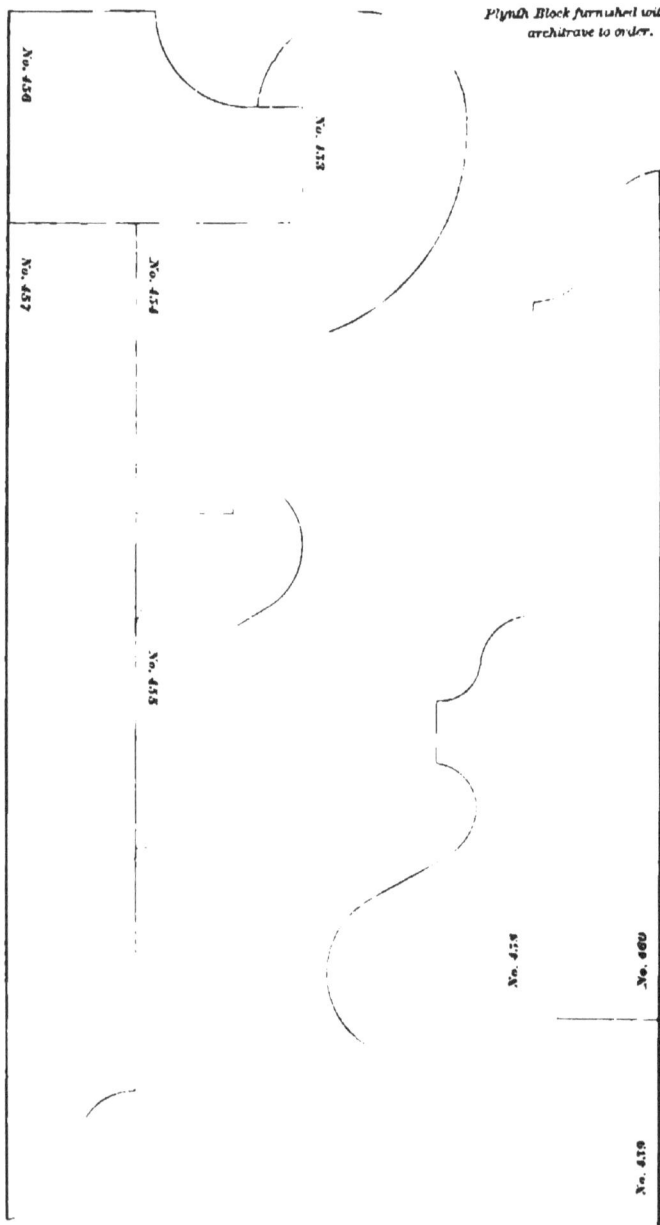

Plynth Block furnished with any architrave to order.

No. 456

No. 453

No. 457

No. 454

No. 455

No. 458

No. 460

No. 459

No. 443

No. 441

No. 164

No. 447

No. 446

No. 449

No. 442

No. 448

Architrave finished out to given
length, extra price.

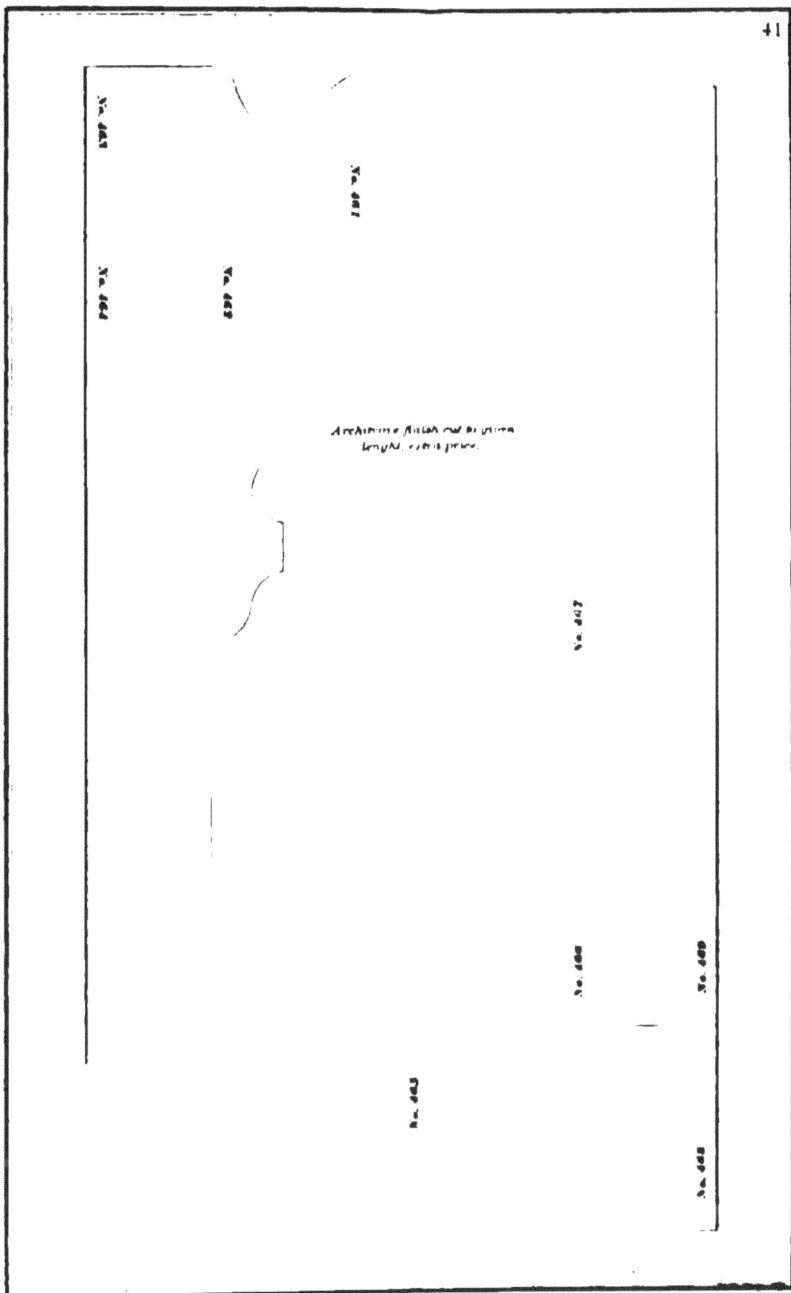

STAIR RAIL.

Stair Rail, — Walnut or Cherry.

No. 470

Stair Rail, — Walnut or Cherry.
Mahogany extra price.

No. 471

No. 472

Cricketing Goods, Croquet and Base Ball, at W. D. McGLOGHLON'S, Jewellery Store, 77 Dundas Street, London, Ont.

No. 474

No. 473

No. 475

Stair Rail.—Walnut or Cherry.

No. 476

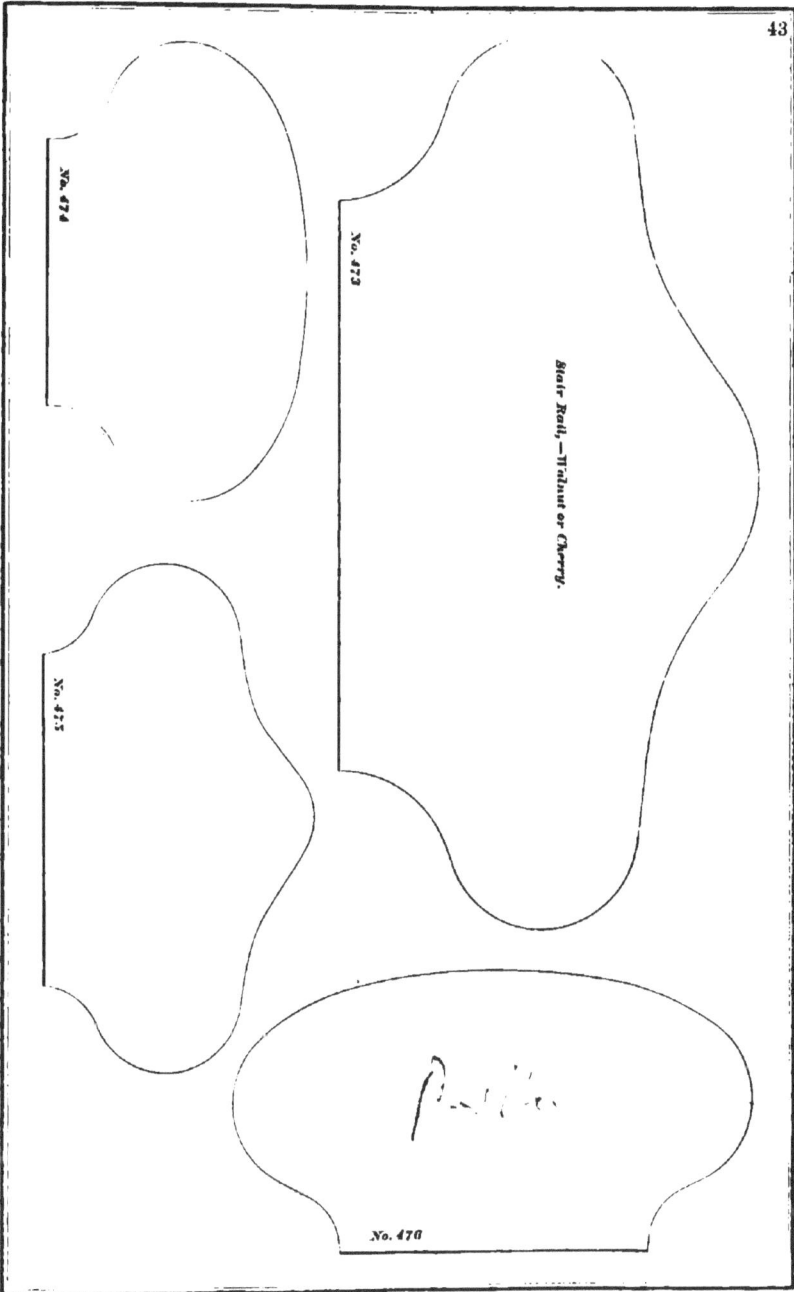

44

No. 477

Stair Rail, — Walnut or Cherry.

No. 478

No. 479

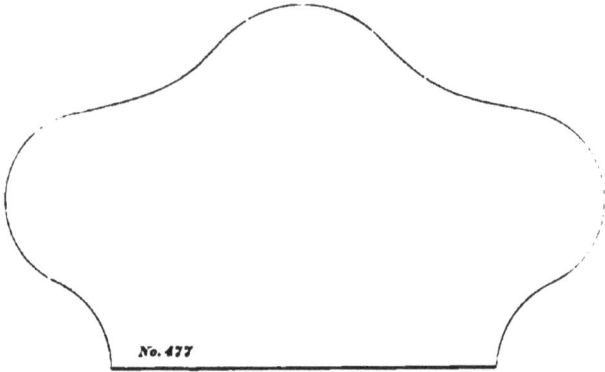

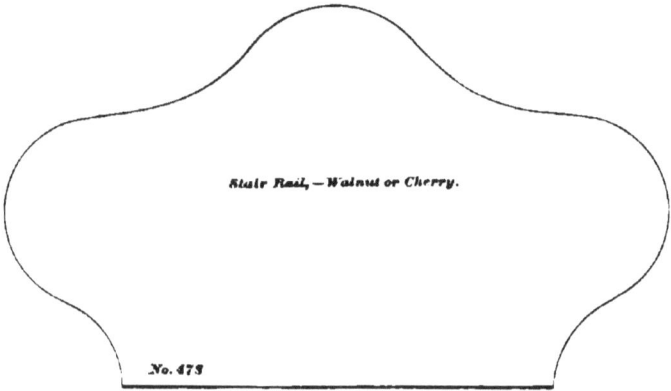

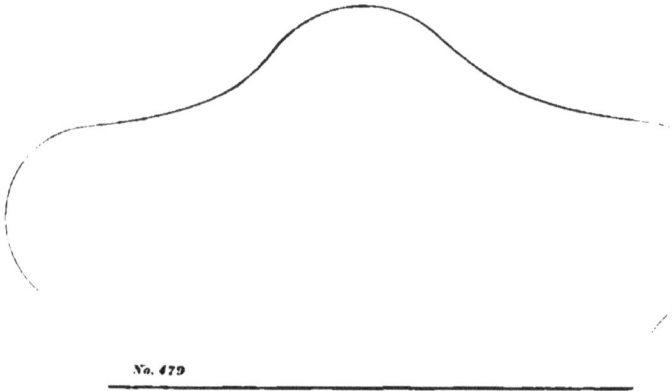

No. 480

Stair Rail.—Walnut or Cherry. Mahogany extra price.

Sent Railing of Hard or Soft Wood.

No. 481

No. 482

Black Walnut

Back of Set

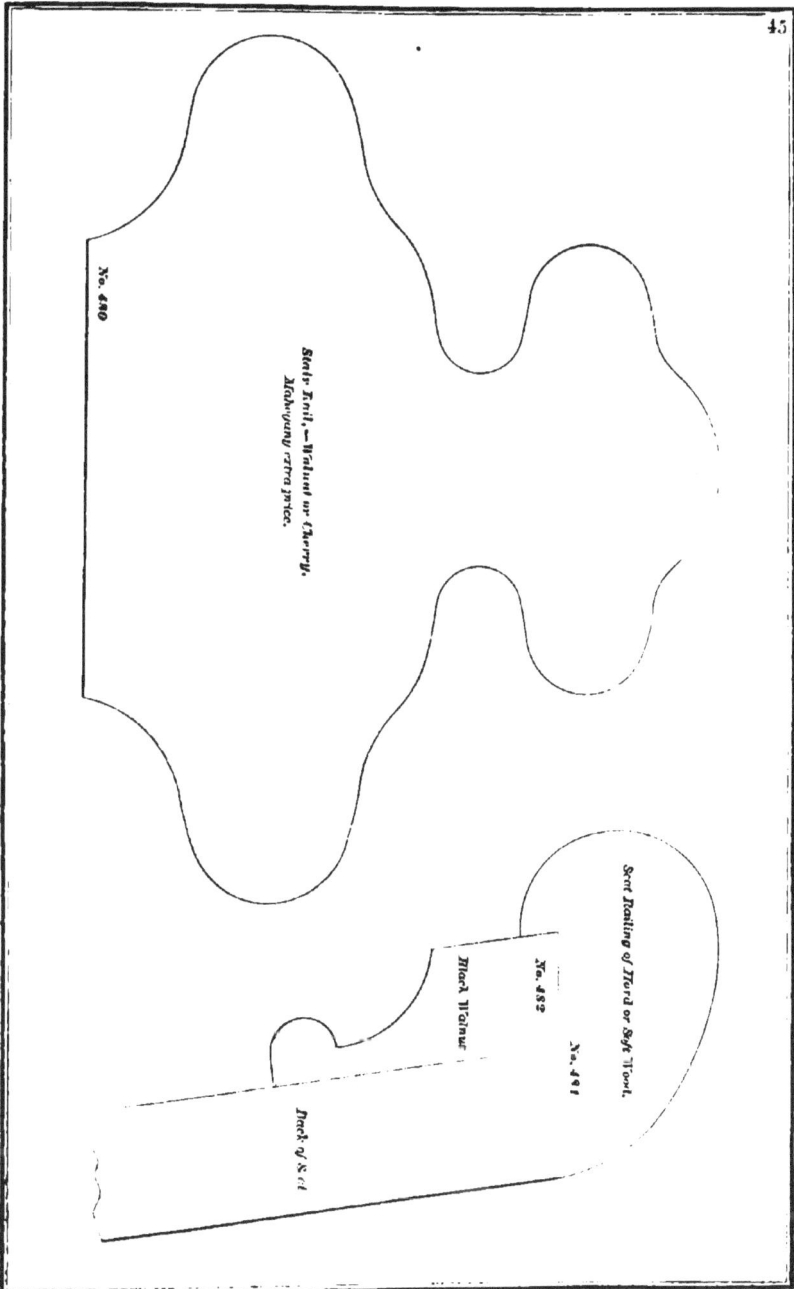

46

Pew back Rail; Walnut, Cherry or Oak.

No. 483

Pew back Rail; Walnut, Cherry or Oak.

No. 484

Pew back Rail; Walnut, Cherry, or Oak.

No. 485

Pew back Rail; Walnut, Cherry or Oak.

No. 486

Pew back Rail; Walnut, Cherry or Oak.

No. 487

Pew Arm, Walnut, Cherry or Oak.

No. 488

Partition Cap; Hard or Soft Wood.

No. 489

Ceiling for Wainscoting, in Walnut, Cherry or Ash.

No. 490

Pew back Rail; Walnut, Cherry or Oak

Flooring, in Walnut, Cherry or Ash.

No. 491

No. 492

No. 493

No. 494

No. 495

No. 496

No. 497

No. 498

No. 499

No. 500

No. 501

No. 502

No. 503

No. 504

No. 505

No. 506

No. 507

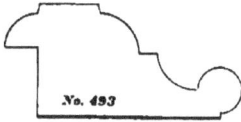

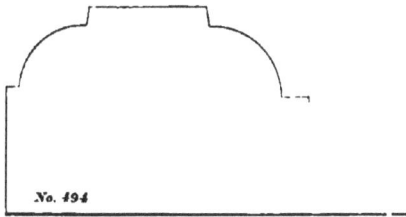

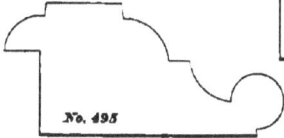

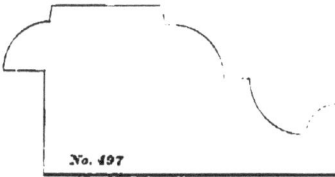

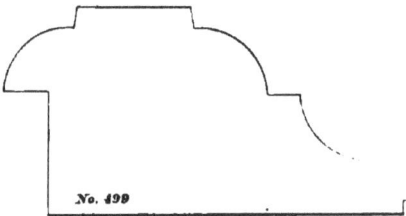

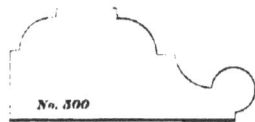

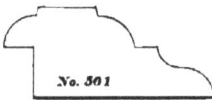

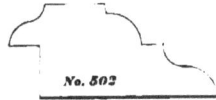

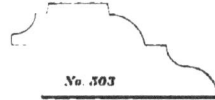

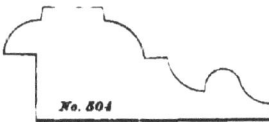

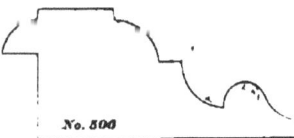

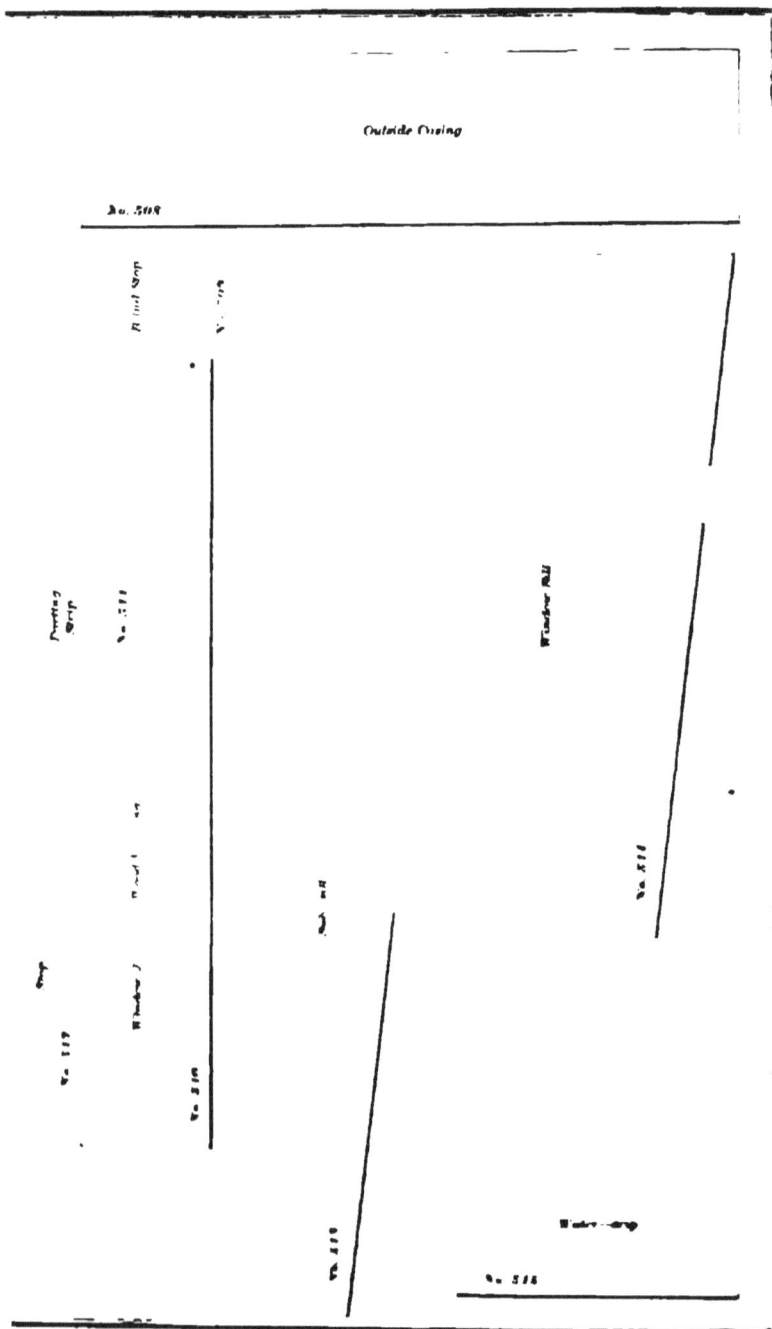

WINDOW FRAME.

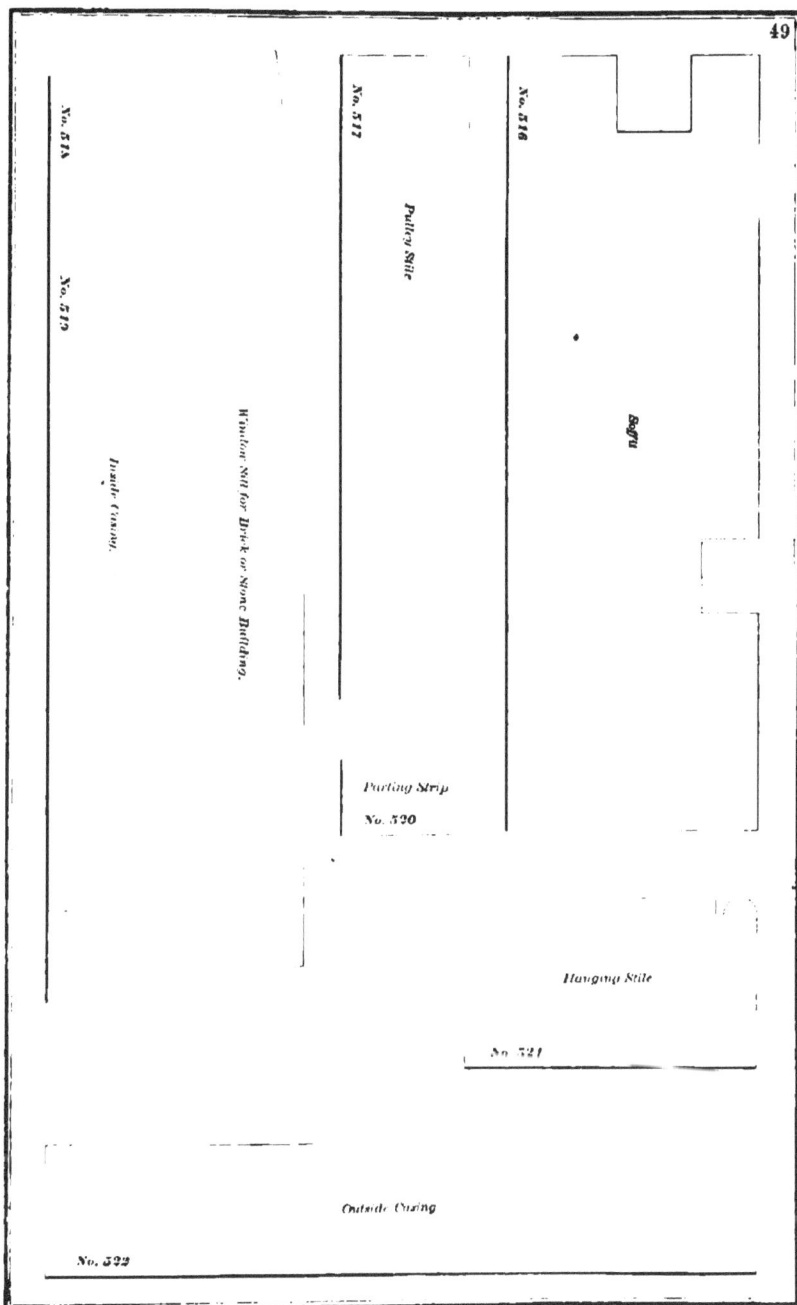

No. 518

No. 519

No. 517

No. 516

Pulley Stile

Window Sill for Brick or Stone Building.

Inside Casing.

Sash

Parting Strip

No. 520

Hanging Stile

No. 521

Outside Casing

No. 522

W. D. McCloghlon repairs all kinds of Clocks, Watches and Jewellery and

Nos. 523 to 569 Dropped.

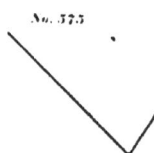

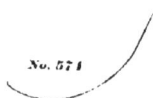

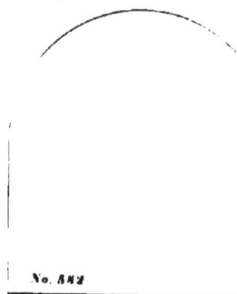

No. 570

No. 572   No. 573

No. 575

No. 571

No. 576   No. 577

No. 574

No. 578   No. 579

No. 580   No. 581   No. 582

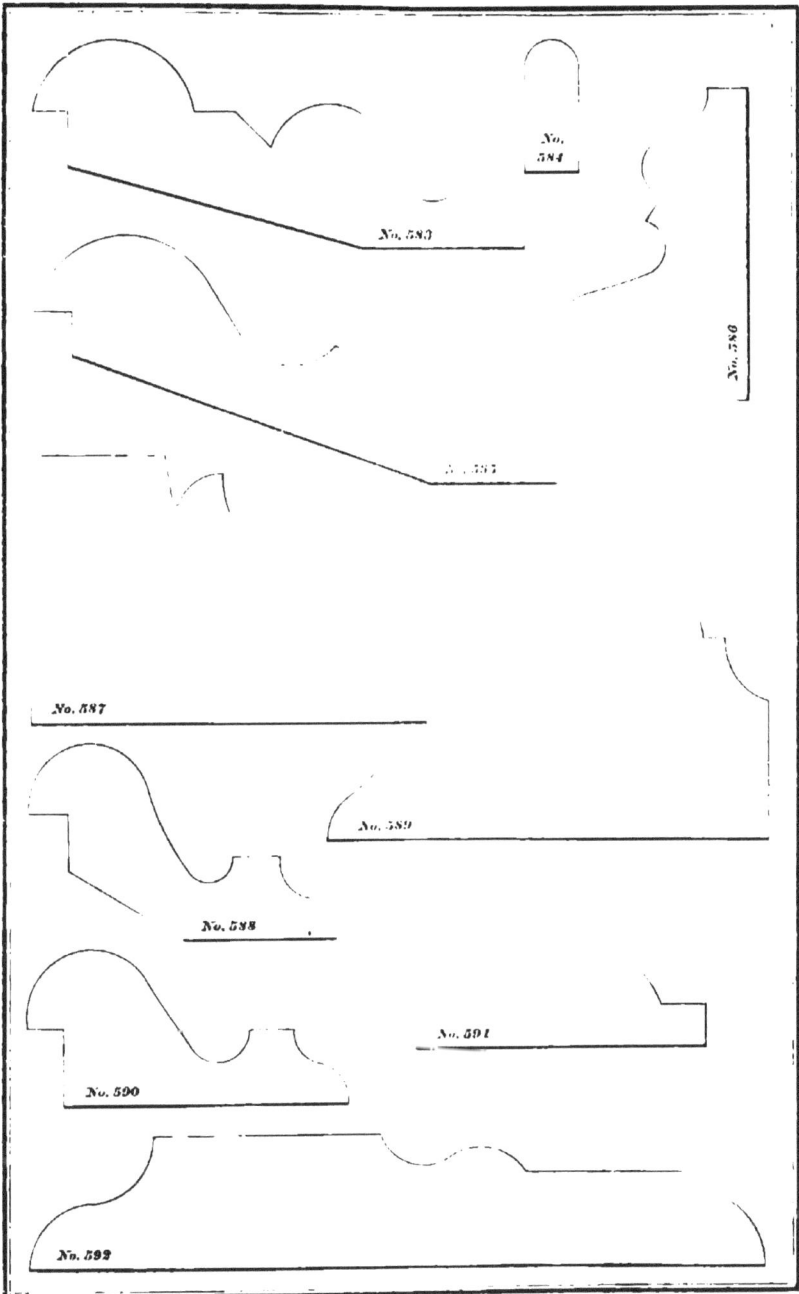

No. 584

No. 583

No. 586

No. 585

No. 587

No. 589

No. 588

No. 591

No. 590

No. 592

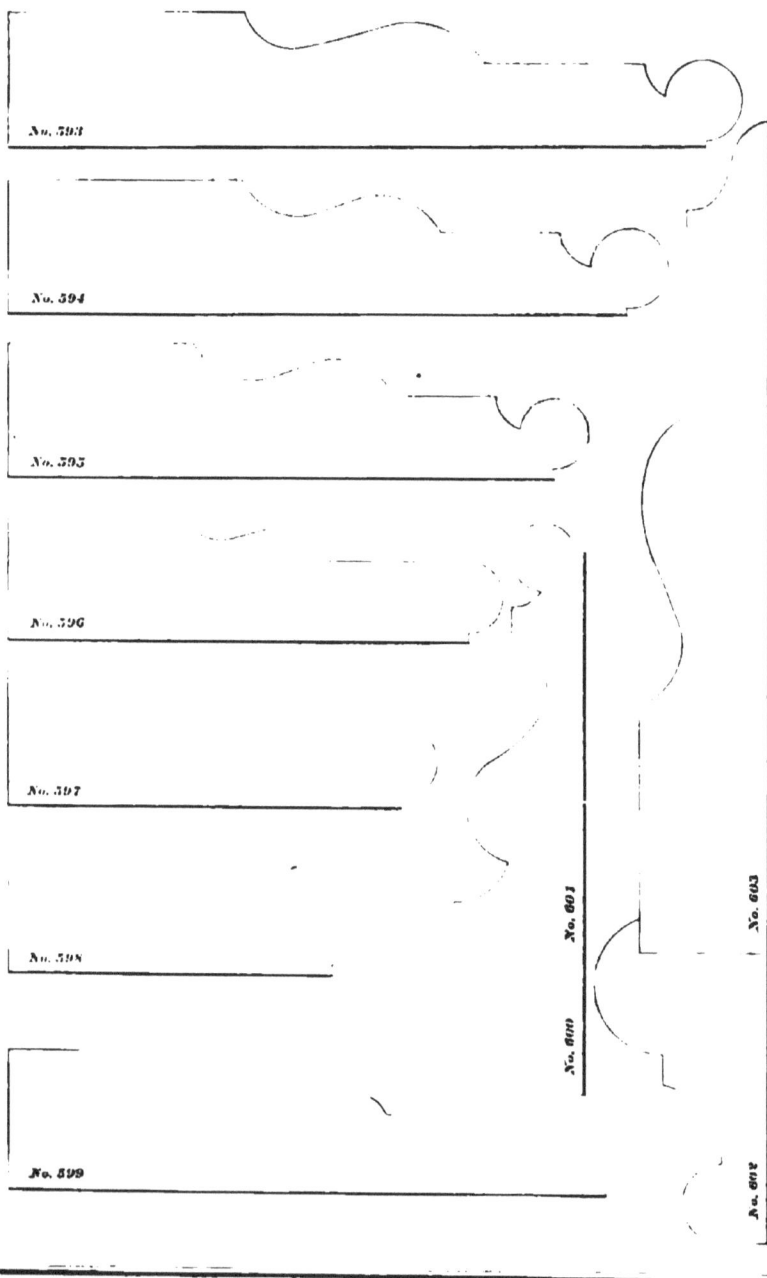

No. 593

No. 594

No. 595

No. 596

No. 597

No. 598

No. 600

No. 601

No. 602

No. 603

No. 599

No. 604

No. 605

No. 606

No. 607

No. 608

No. 609

No. 610

No. 614

No. 612

No. 613

No. 611

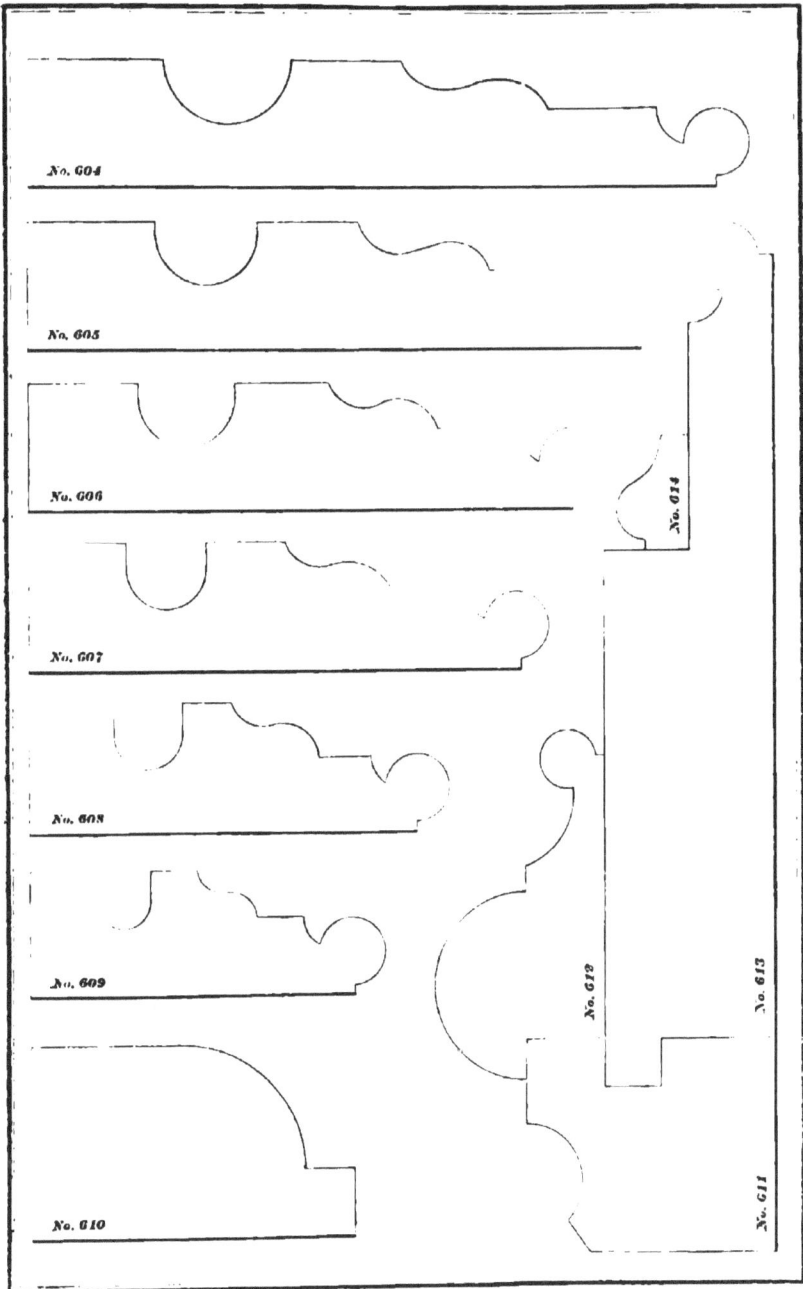

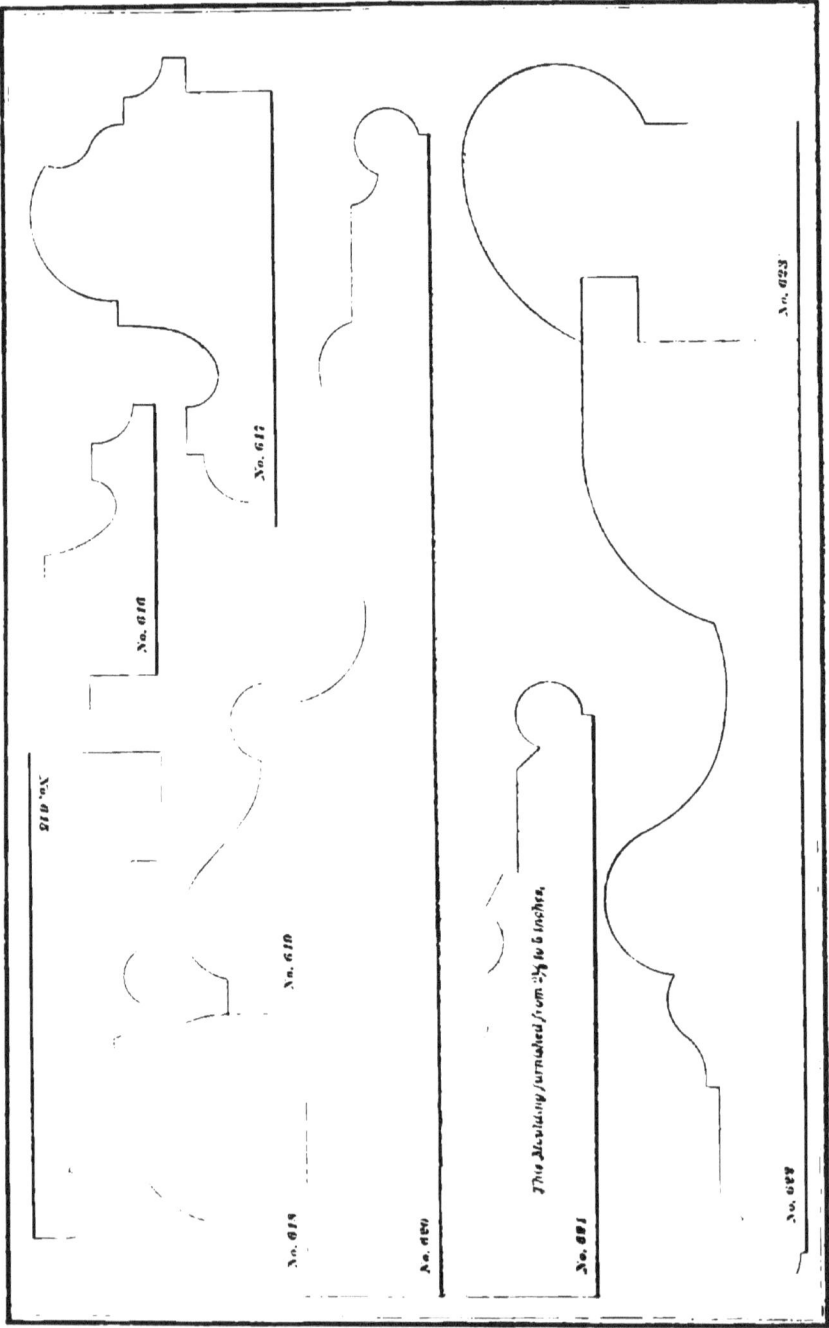

No. 617

No. 616

No. 615

No. 619

No. 614

No. 620

This Moulding furnished from 2½ to 6 inches.

No. 621

No. 623

No. 622

No. 627

No. 624

No. 626

No. 625

No. 628

No. 629

No. 635

No. 636

No. 630

No. 631

No. 634

No. 632

No. 633

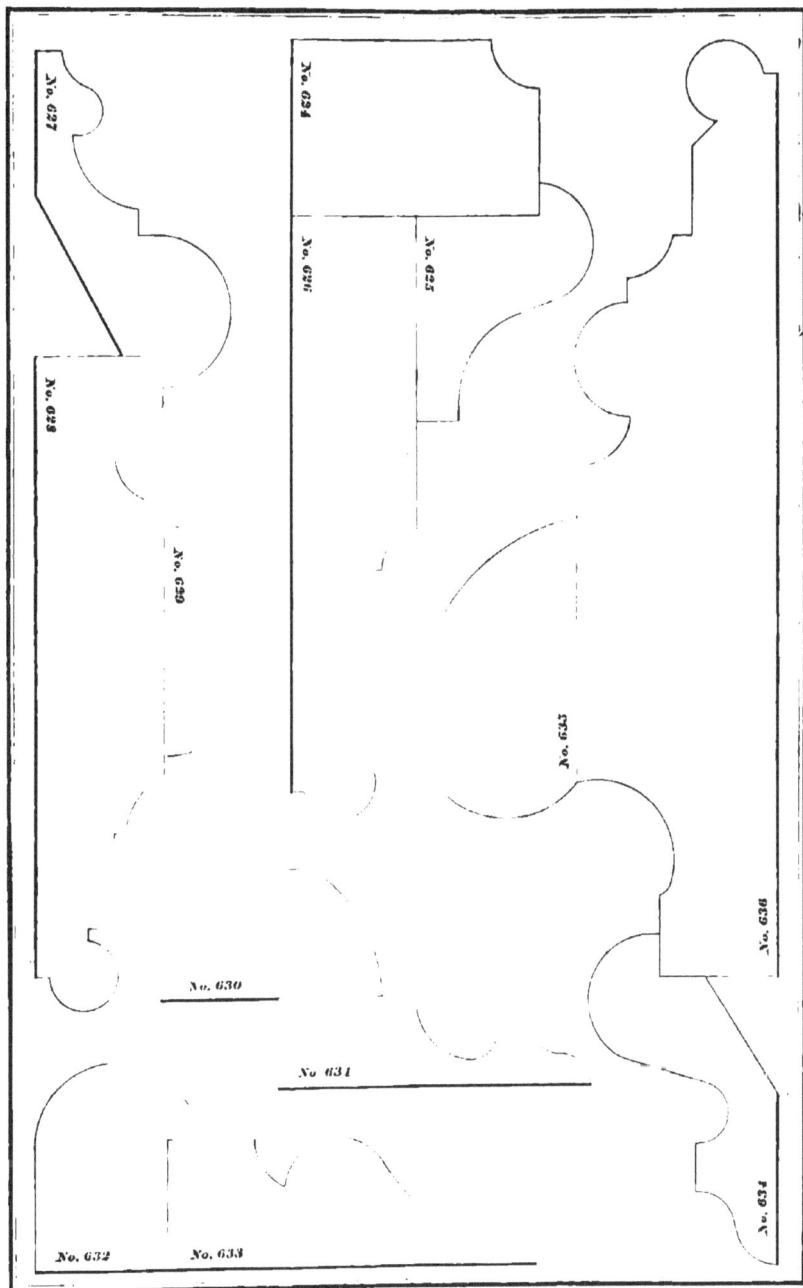

W. D. McGloghlon repairs all kinds of Clocks, Watches and Jewellery and guarantees satisfaction.

No. 664

No. 663

No. 662

No. 661

No. 660

No. 659

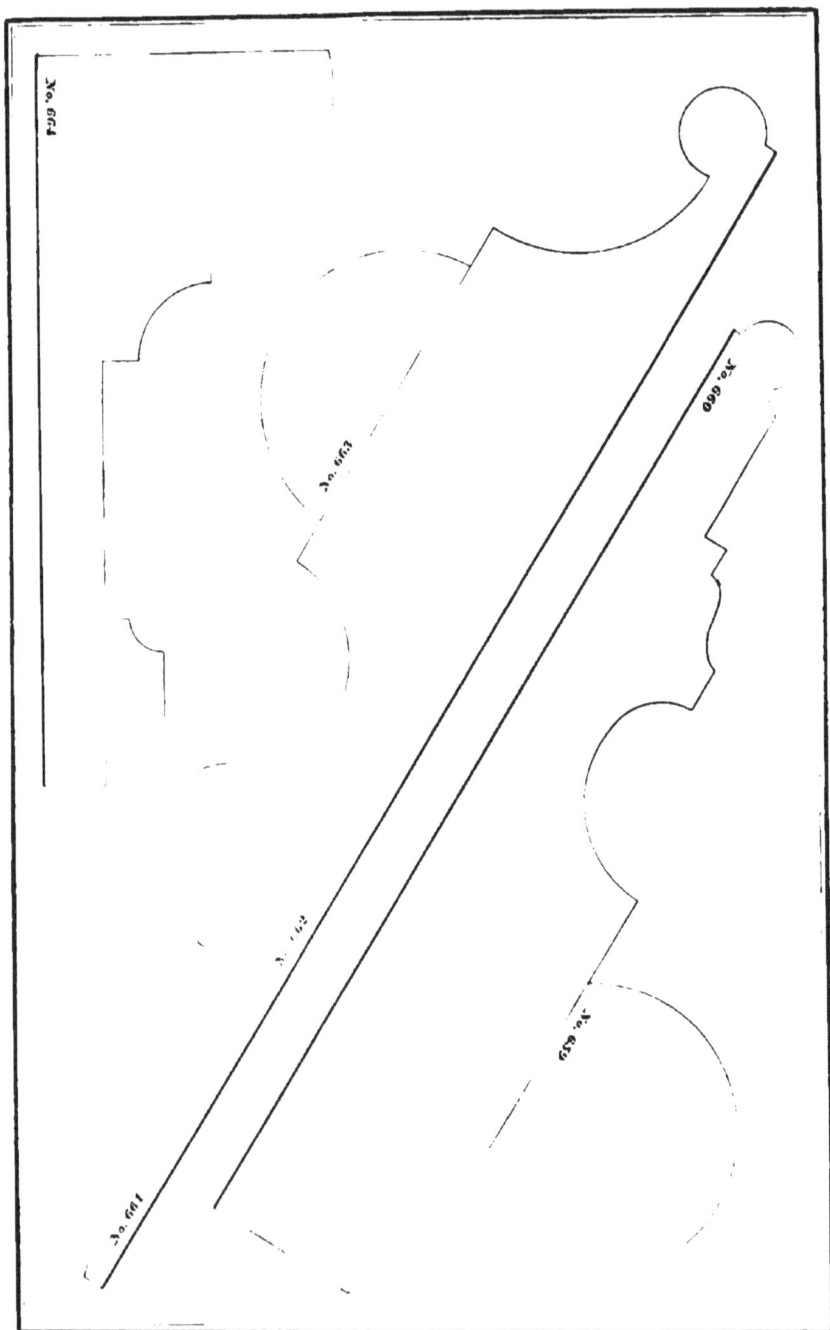

Segment Head Broken Box-Cap Door Frame, made with Plain or Paneled Jambs,
For Wood Building.

Fig. B.

Transom Light.

Broken Box-Cap Window Frames made to correspond, Doors made any Style desired.
For Section of Frame, see page 84, Fig. 38.

The Handsomest and Finest Jewellery Store in the Dominion, 77 Dundas-St.

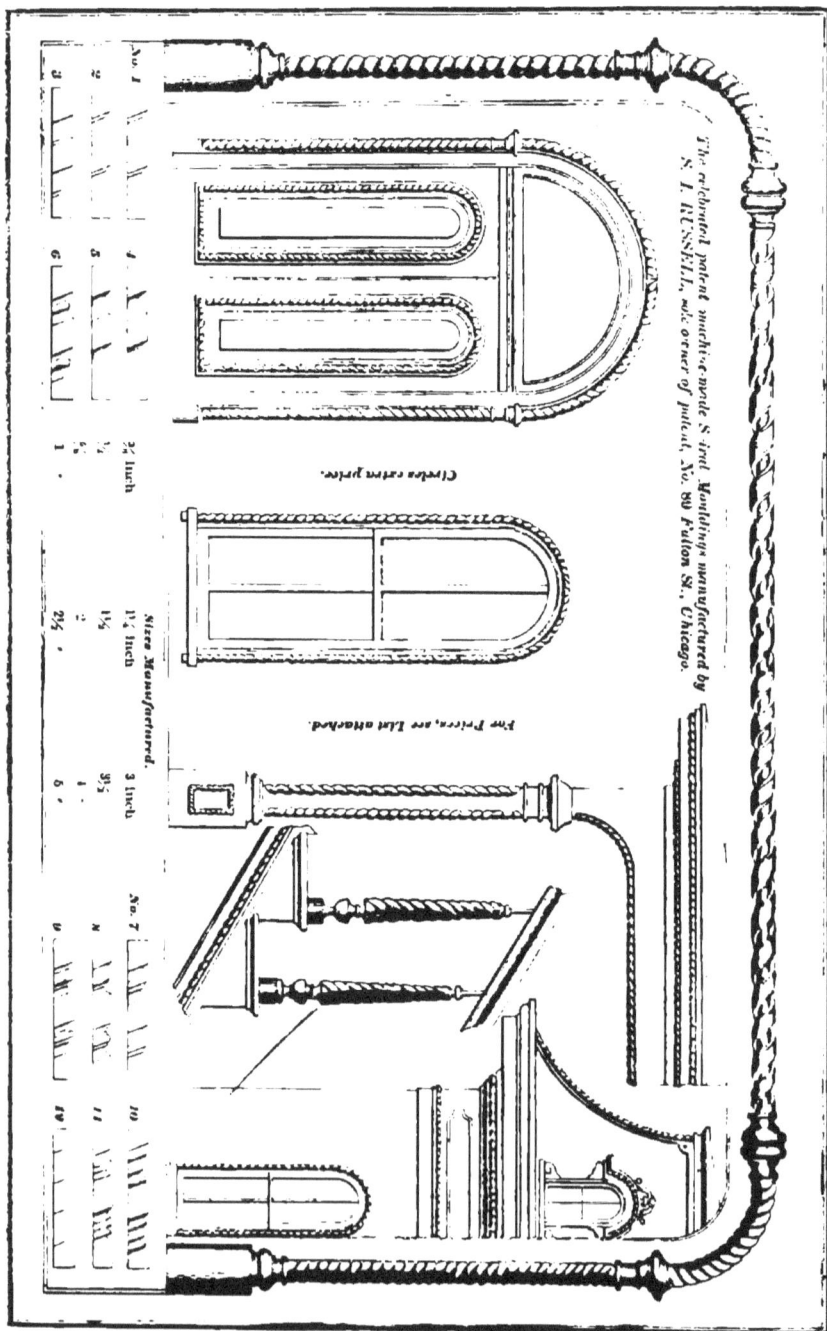

W. D. McGLOGHLON repairs all kinds of Clocks, Watches and Jewellery, and guarantees satisfaction.

No. 1

No. 2

No. 3

No. 4

When ordering Brackets give size and thickness.

No. 5

No. 6

Brackets made any size and thickness.

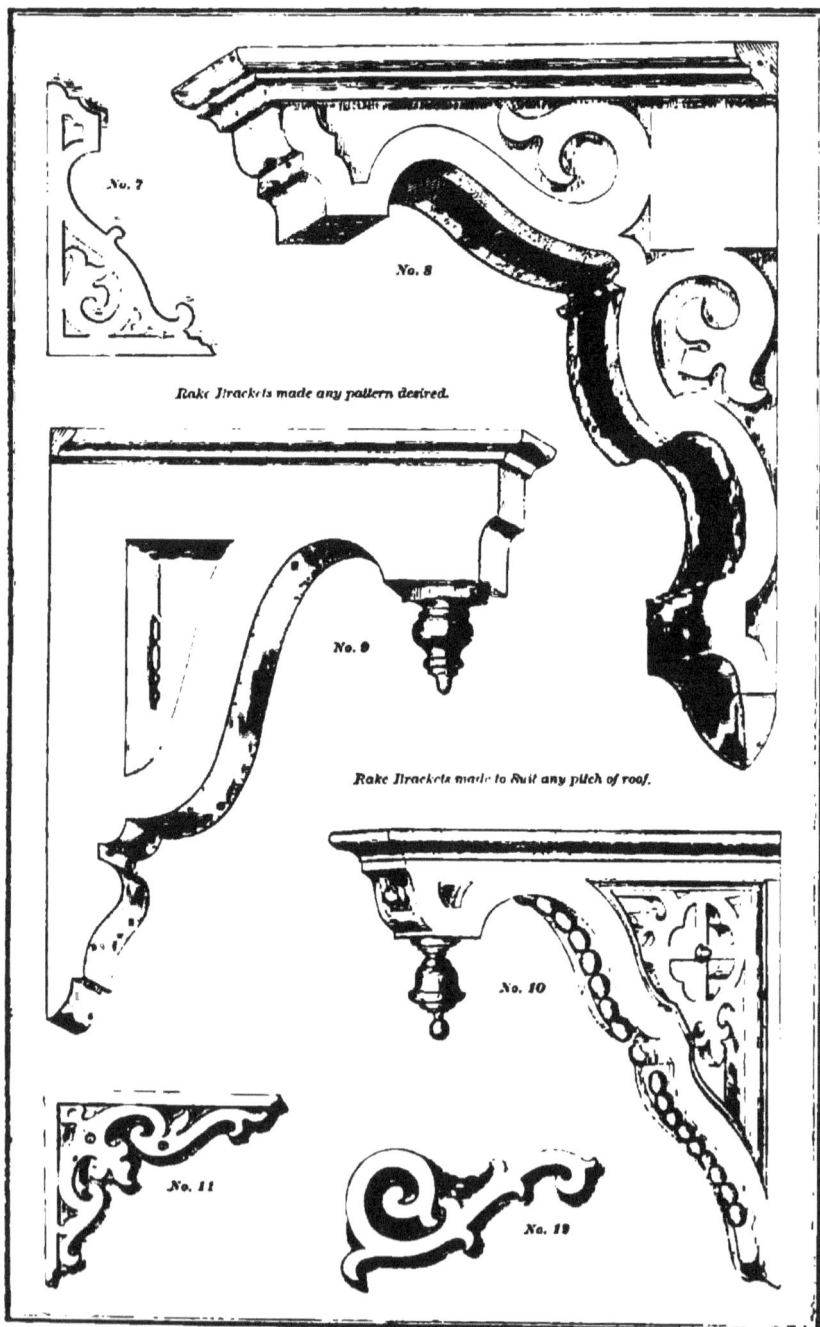

No. 7

No. 8

Rake Brackets made any pattern desired.

No. 9

Rake Brackets made to suit any pitch of roof.

No. 10

No. 11

No. 12

No. 14

No. 13

Brackets made any size and thickness desired.

No. 15

No. 16

No. 17

No. 18

No. 19

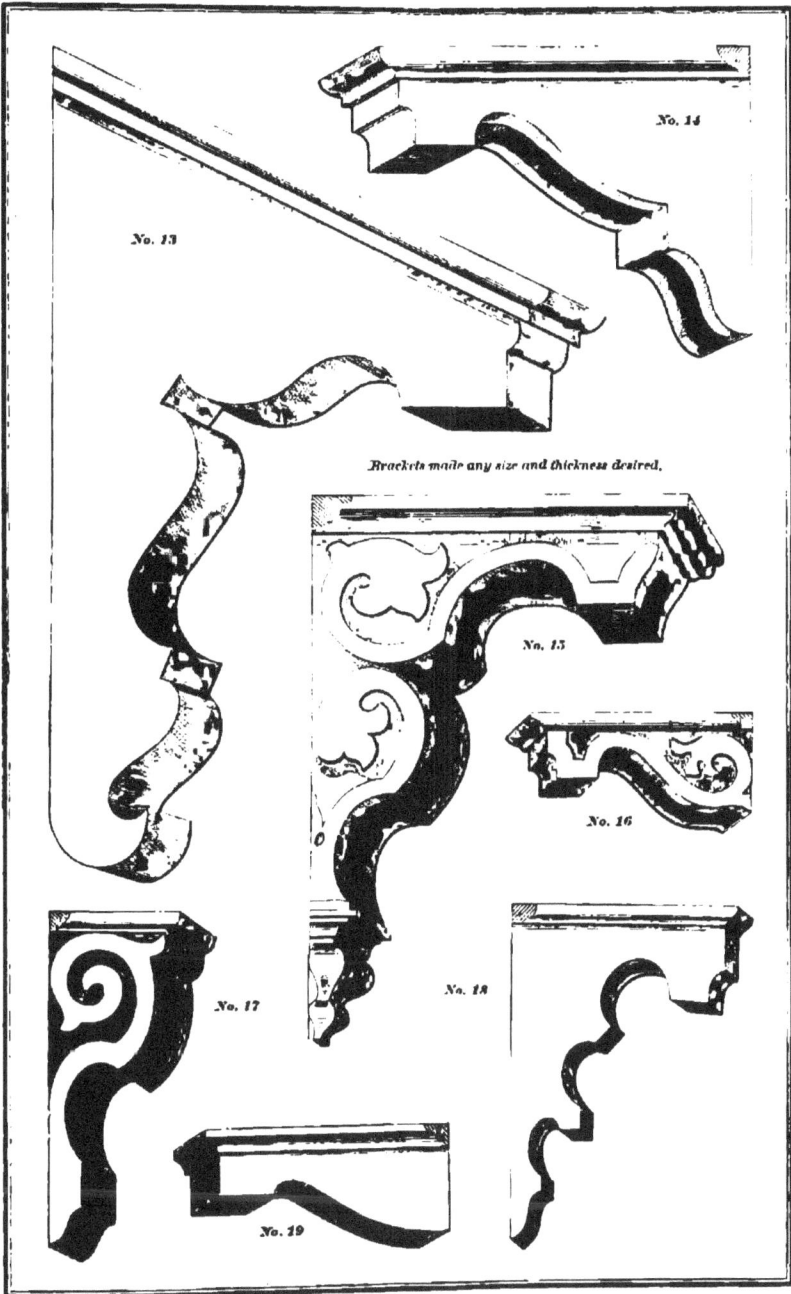

Fine Silver and Plated Ware in Beautiful Tea Setts, Cake Baskets, Cruet Cups, For Spoons. &c.. &c.. at 77 Dundas Street.

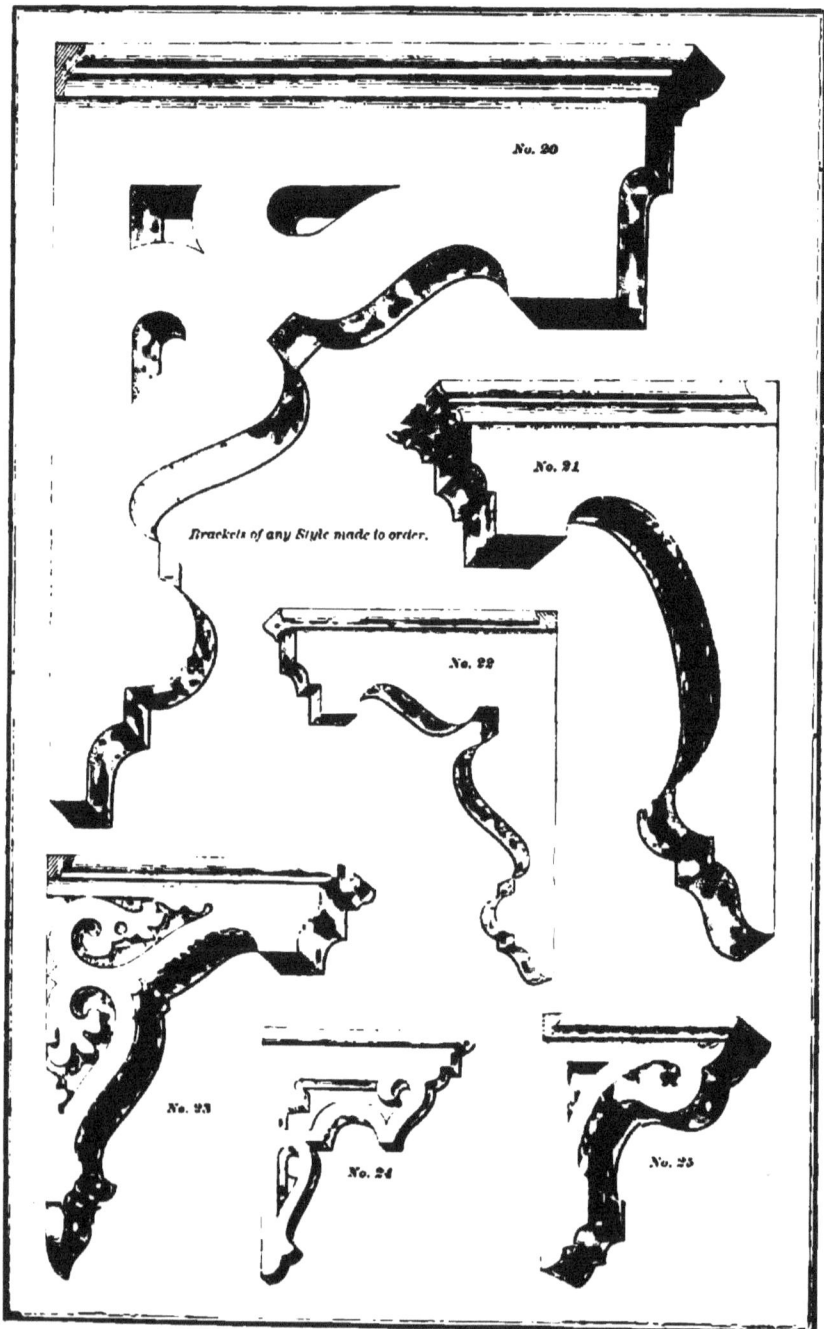

No. 20

No. 21

Brackets of any Style made to order.

No. 22

No. 23

No. 24

No. 25

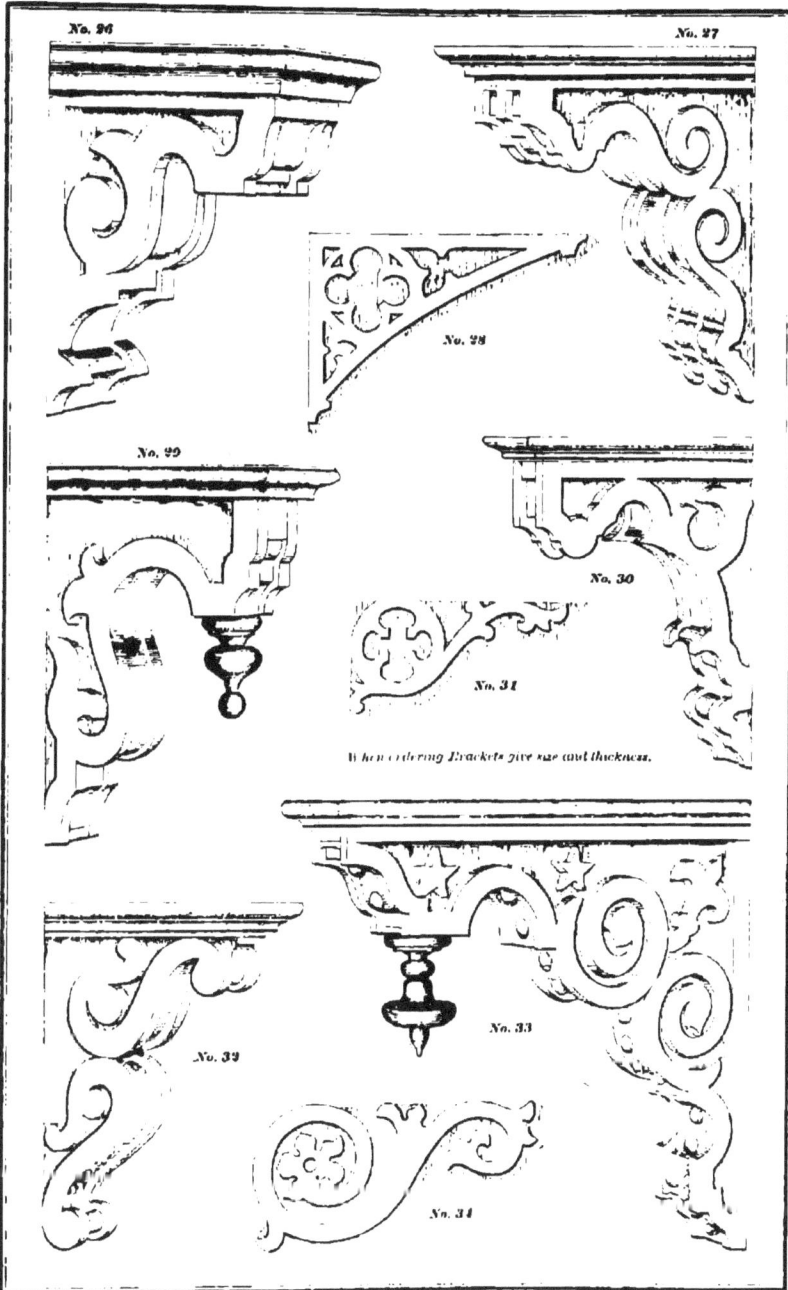

No. 26
No. 27
No. 28
No. 29
No. 30
No. 31

When ordering Brackets give size and thickness.

No. 32
No. 33
No. 34

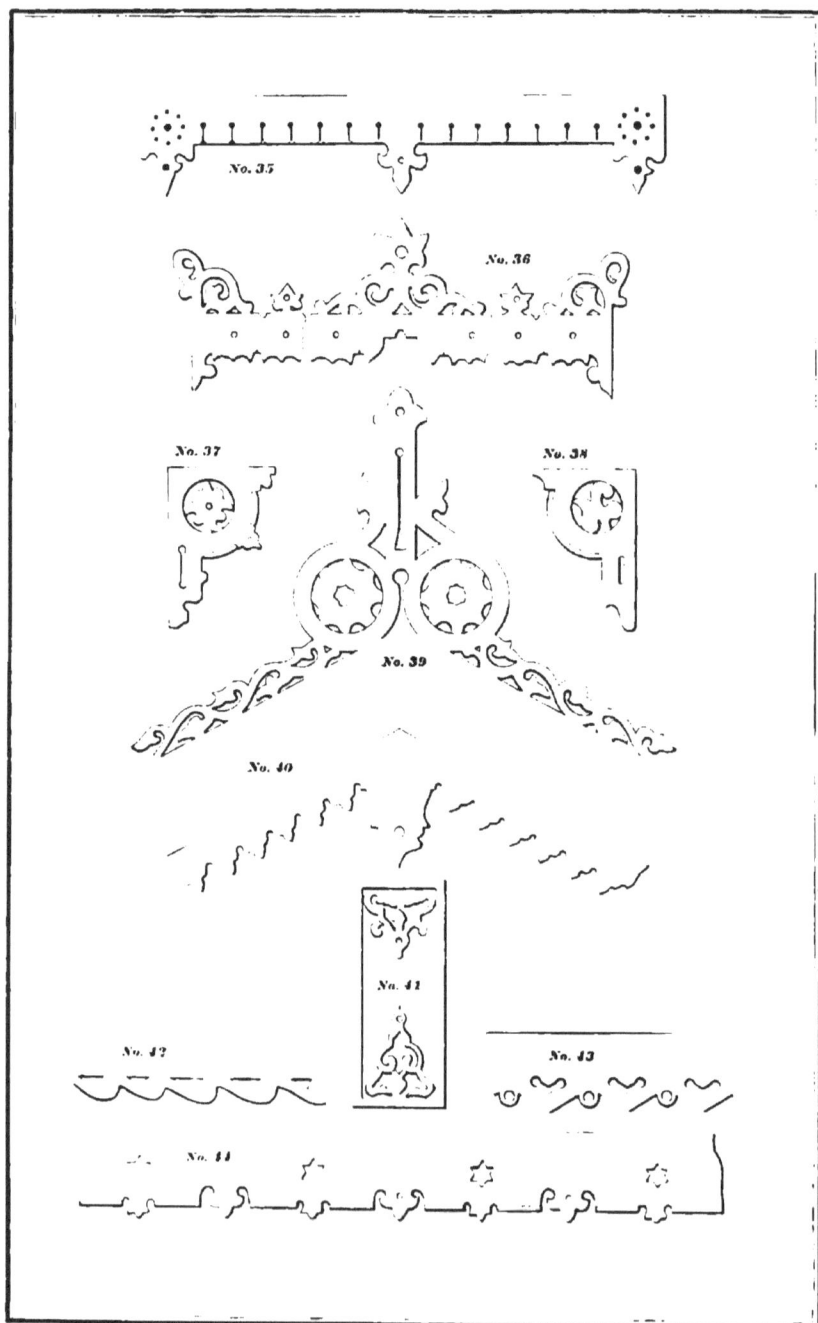

SCROLL WORK.

No. 35

No. 36

No. 37   No. 38

No. 39

No. 40

No. 41

No. 42   No. 43

No. 44

No. 45

No. 46

No. 47

No. 48

No. 49

No. 50

No. 51

No. 52

No. 53

No. 54

No. 55

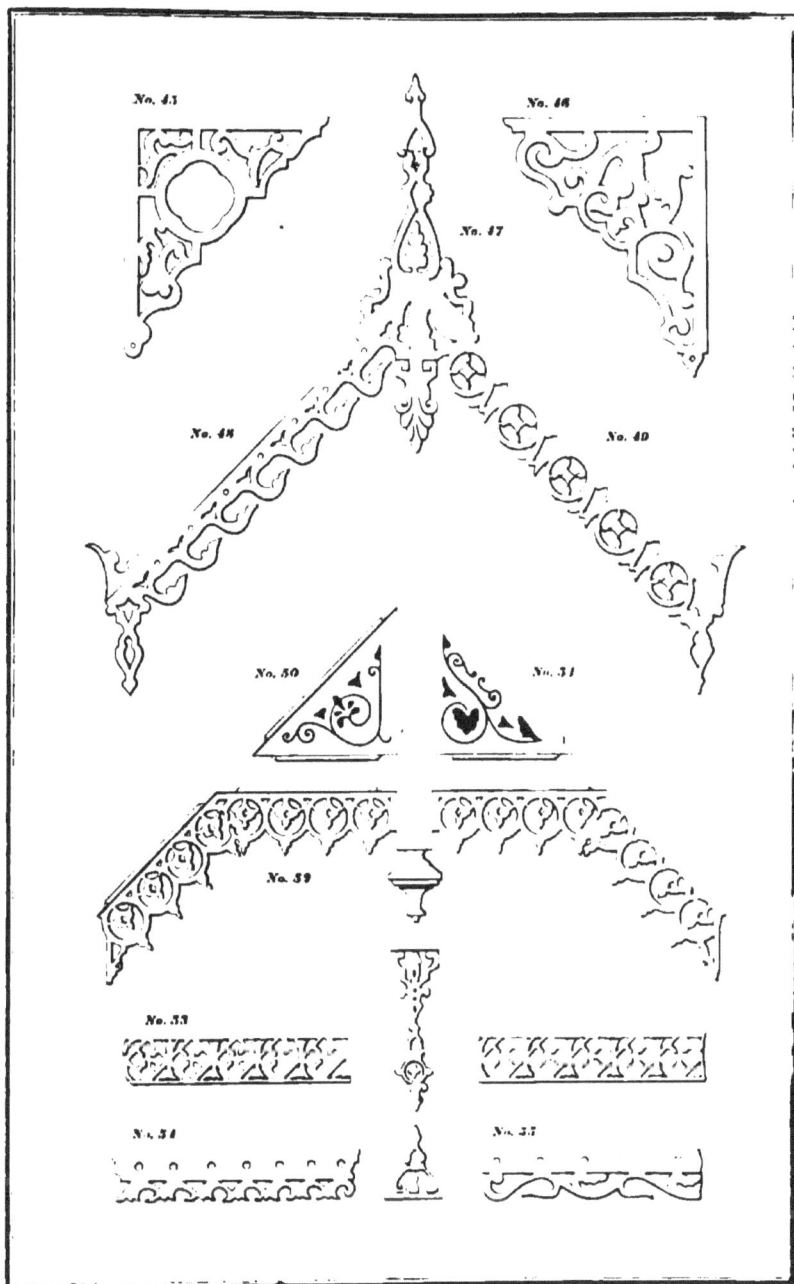

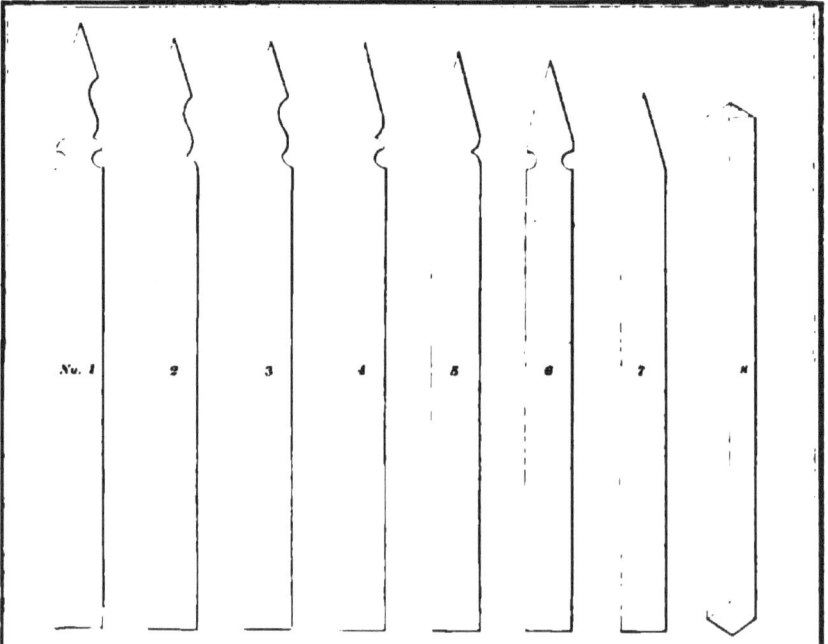

Fence material furnished of every description

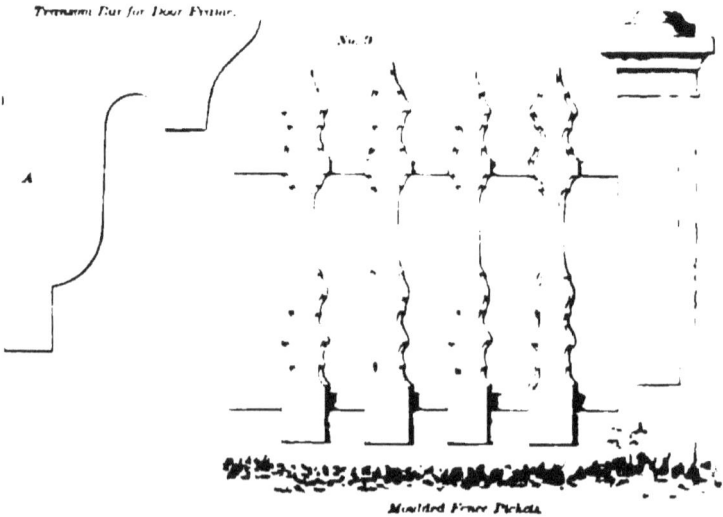

Tenon Bar for Door Frame.

No. 9

A

Moulded Fence Pickets.

No. 1   2   3   4   5   6   7   8

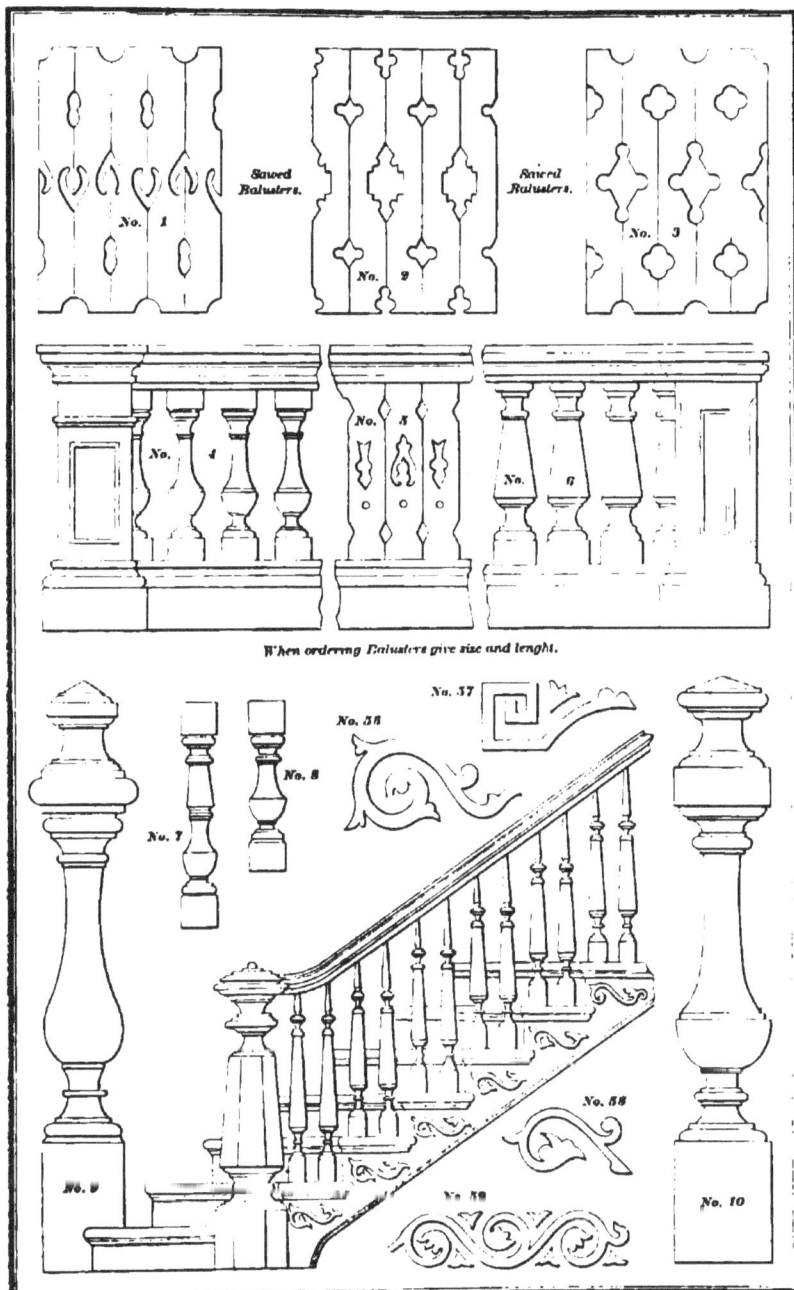

Sawed Balusters. No. 1

No. 2

Sawed Balusters. No. 3

No. 4

No. 5

No. 6

When ordering Balusters give size and lenght.

No. 37

No. 56

No. 8

No. 7

No. 9

No. 55

No. 59

No. 10

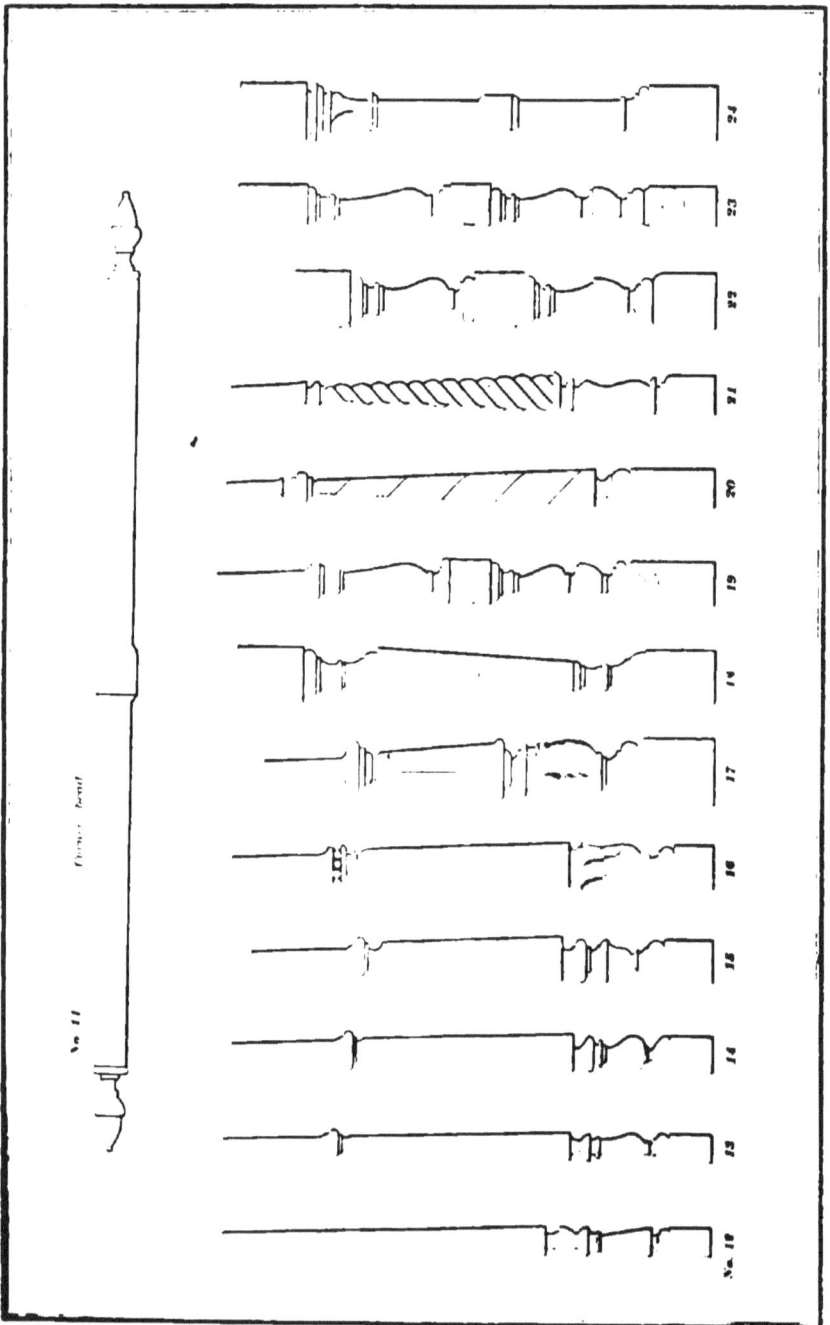

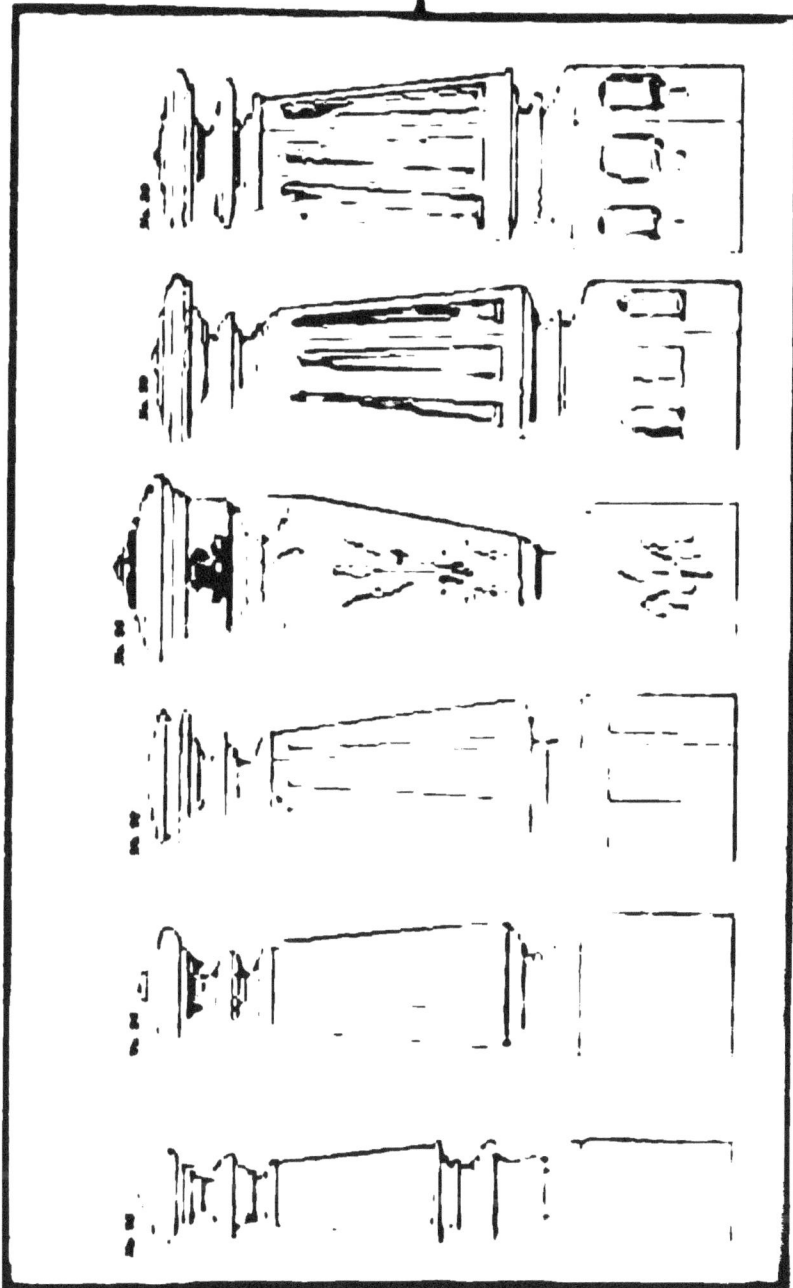

Fig. 1

Fig. 2

Fig. 3

Fig. 4

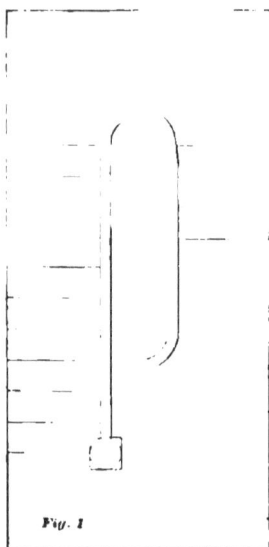

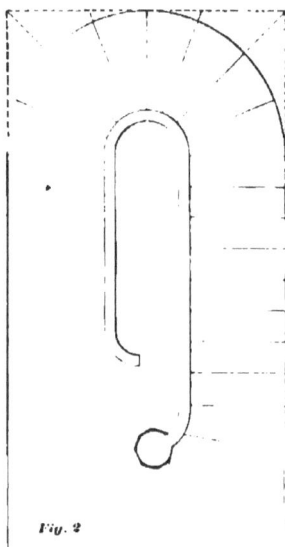

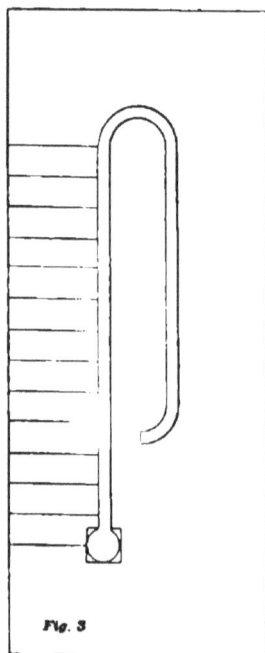

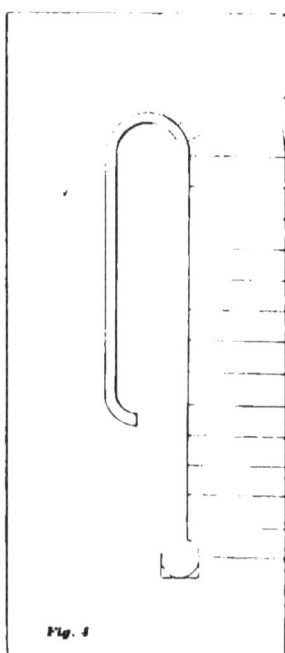

For first-class goods of all kinds go to W. D. McGLOGHLON'S, the best House in the West.

Fig. 5

Fig. 6

Fig. 7

(Inside Doors.)

Fig. 8

Fig. 9

Fig. 10

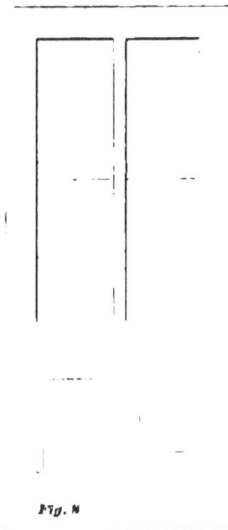

W. D. McGLOGHLON, 77 Dundas Street, keeps constantly on hand the largest, cheapest stock in the City.

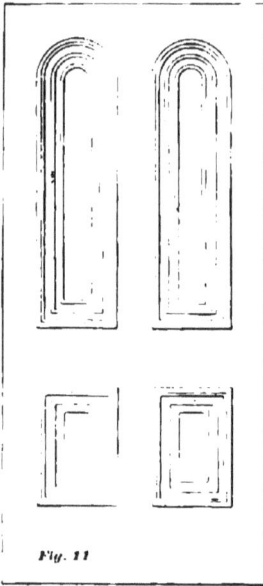

Front Doors.

Fig. 11   *Fig. 12*

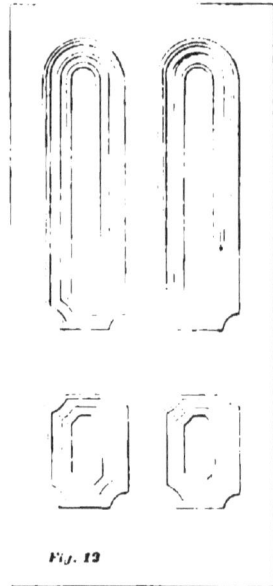

Doors furnished any number of Panels desired.

Fig. 13   *Fig. 14*

Inside Door.   *Sliding or Folding Doors.*

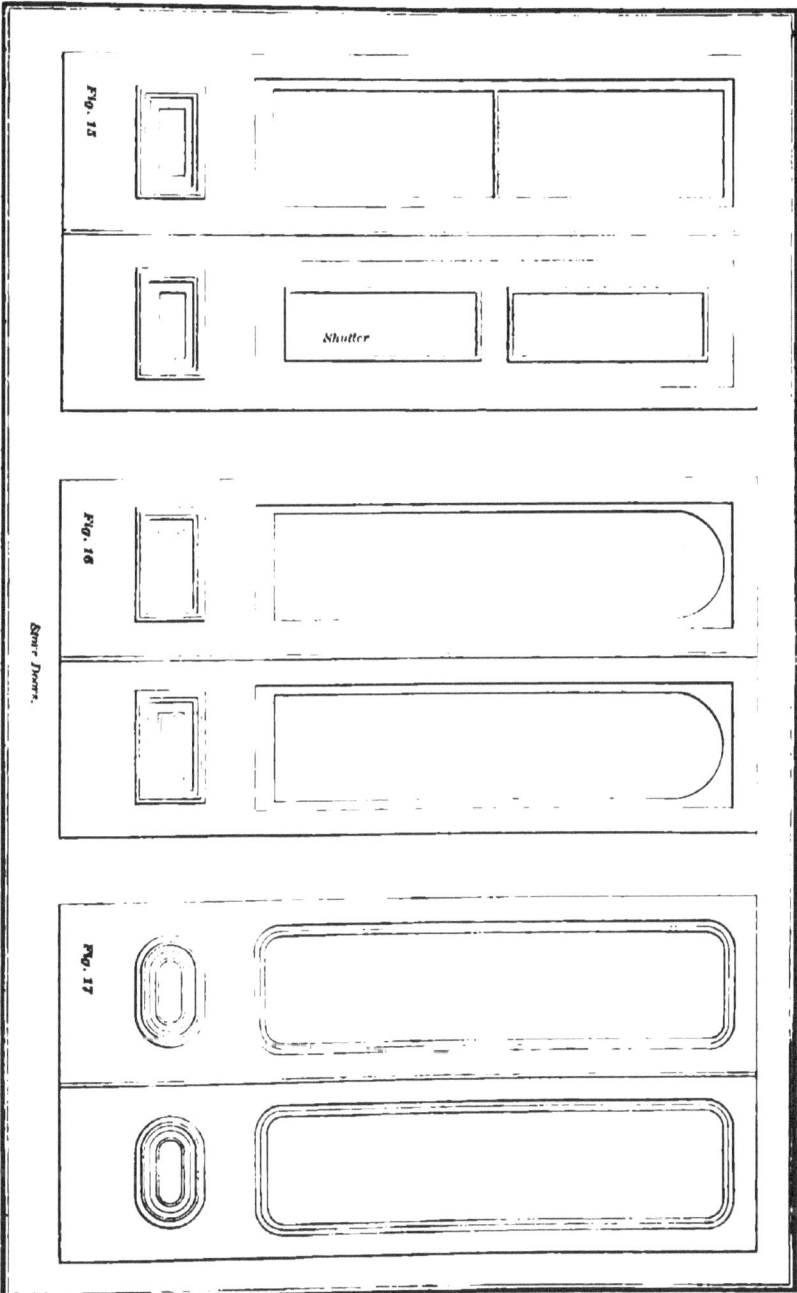

Fig. 15

Shutter

Fig. 16

Store Doors.

Fig. 17

The Fairchild Gold Pens took First Prizes and Gold Medals, at Paris and Vienna World's Fairs.

Segment-head Box-cap Door-frame, made with Plain or Paneled Jambs.
For Wood Building.

Fig. 14

Transom light.

For section of Frame see page 84, *Fig. 88.*

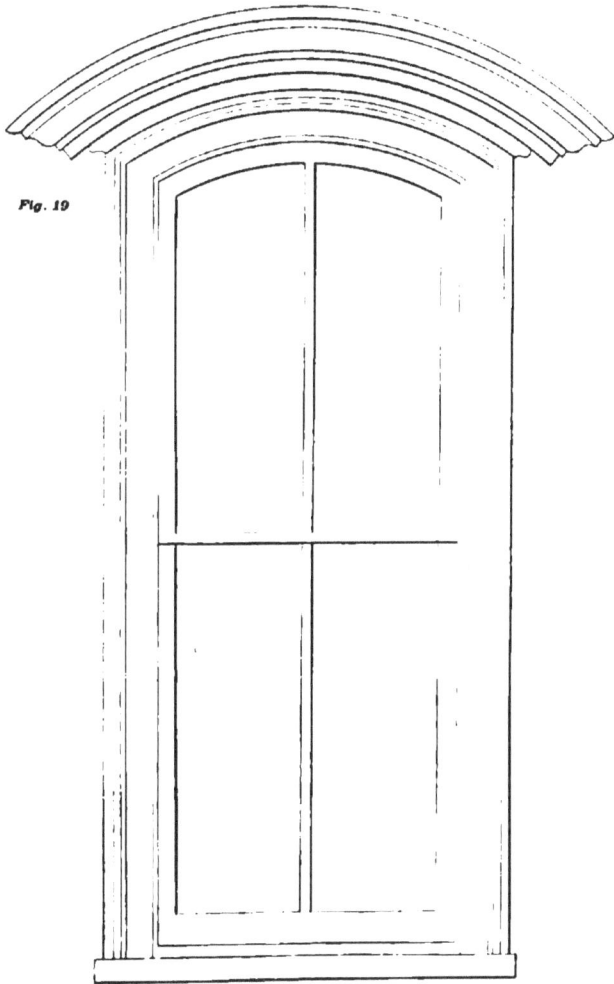

Segment-head Box-cap Window-frame, made with Pulleys for weights.

For Wood Building.

Fig. 19

For section of Frame see page 84, Fig. 37.

W. D. McGLOGHLON, 77 Dundas Street, keeps constantly on hand the largest, cheapest stock in the City

Door Frame with front and vestibule doors.

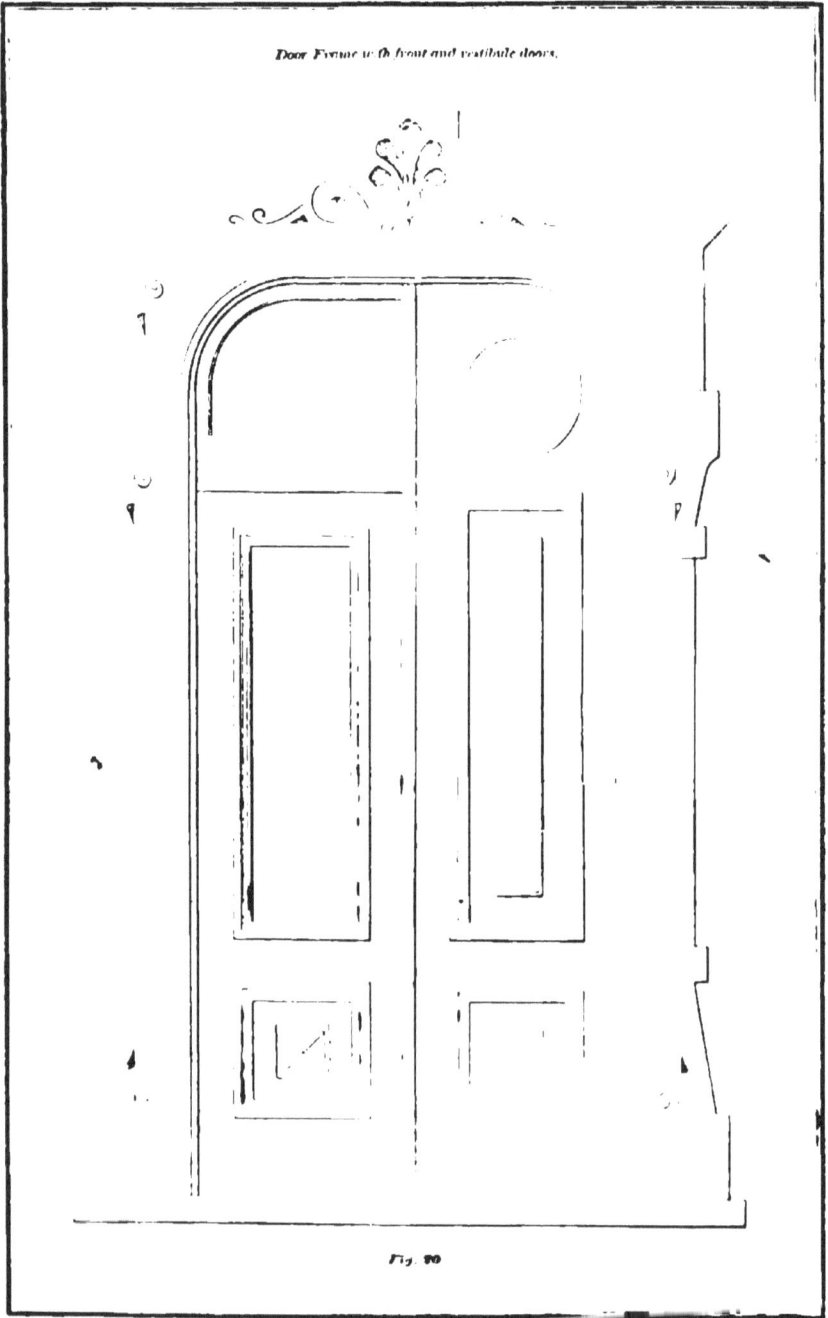

Fig. 80

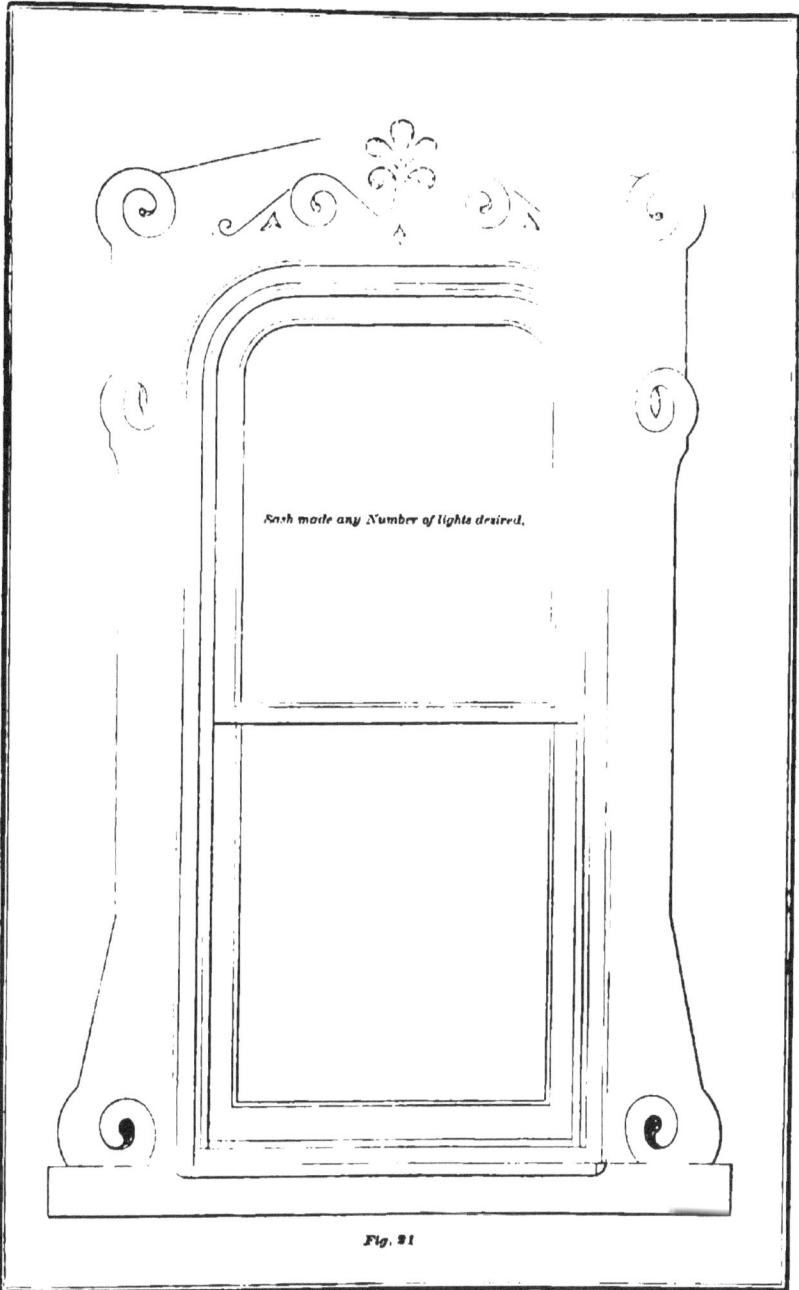

Sash made any Number of lights desired.

Fig. 21

DOOR FRAME.

Semi-circle frame for Brick or Stone Building with Rope Moulding.

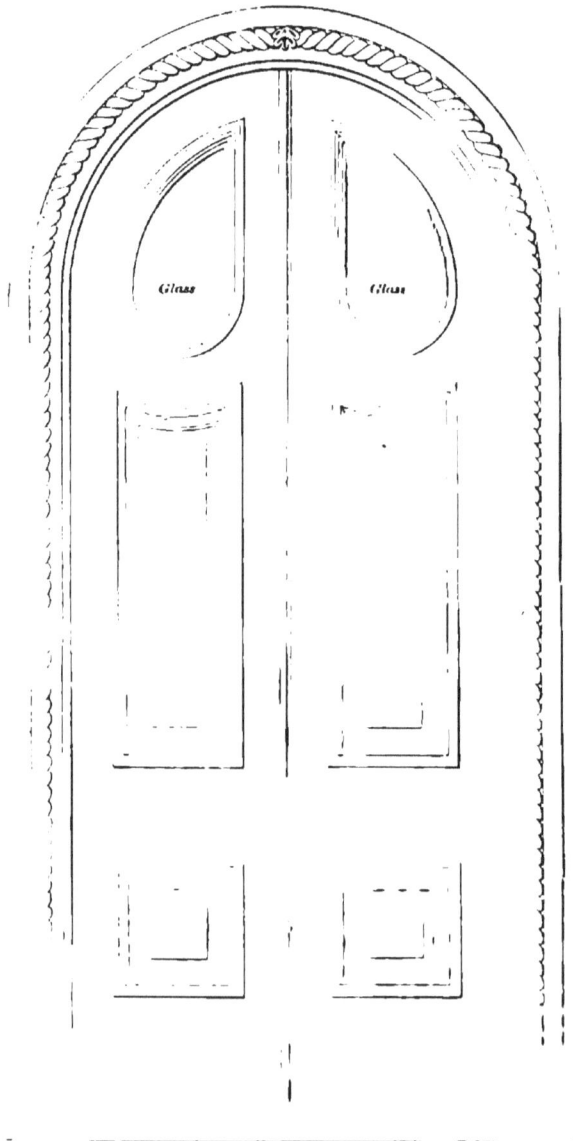

Glass   Glass

Half-circle frame for Brick or Stone Building — Faça Moulding.

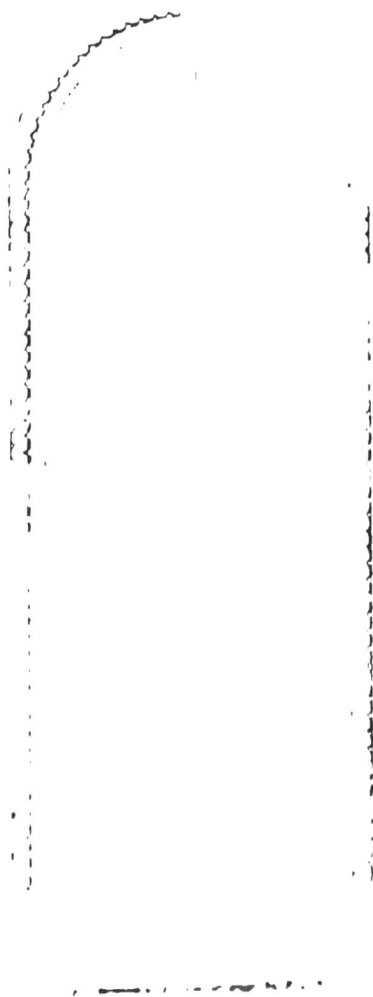

Fig. 93

Reversible back Pew end.

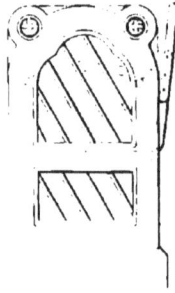

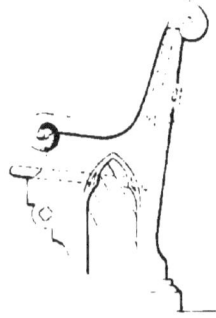

Fig. 24

Fig. 25

Fig. 26

Pew ends furnished, any design.

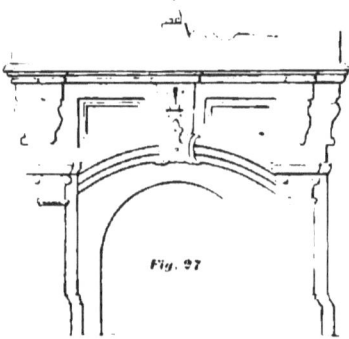

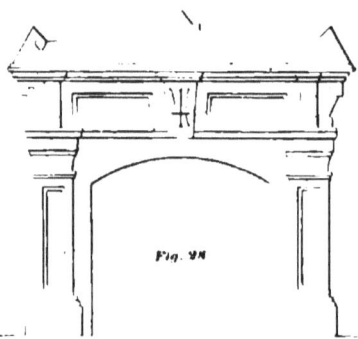

Fig. 27

Fig. 28

Wood Mantles.

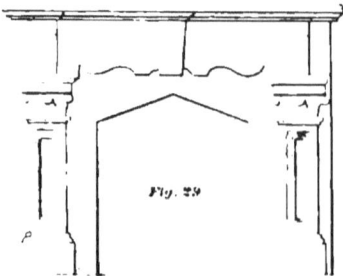

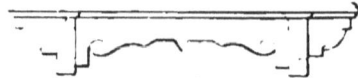

Fig. 30

Mantle Shelves.

Fig. 29

Fig. 31

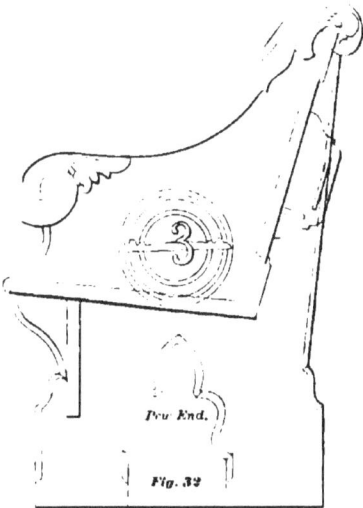

Pew End.

Fig. 32

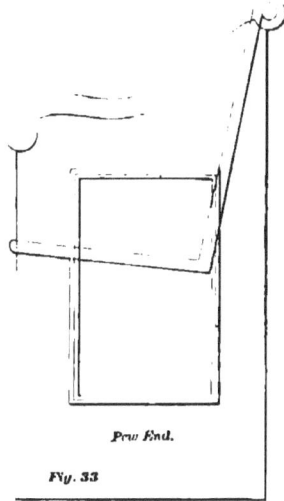

Pew End.

Fig. 33

Church Seats made with Black-walnut, Cherry or Mahogany Back-roll and partition Cup, ready to put together.

Pew ends furnished Complete.

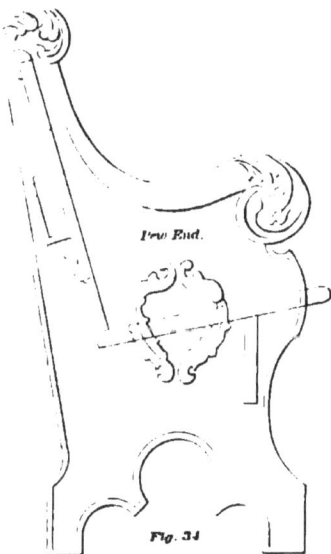

Pew End.

Fig. 34

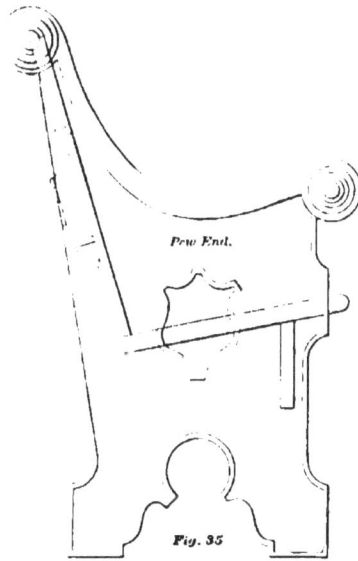

Pew End.

Fig. 35

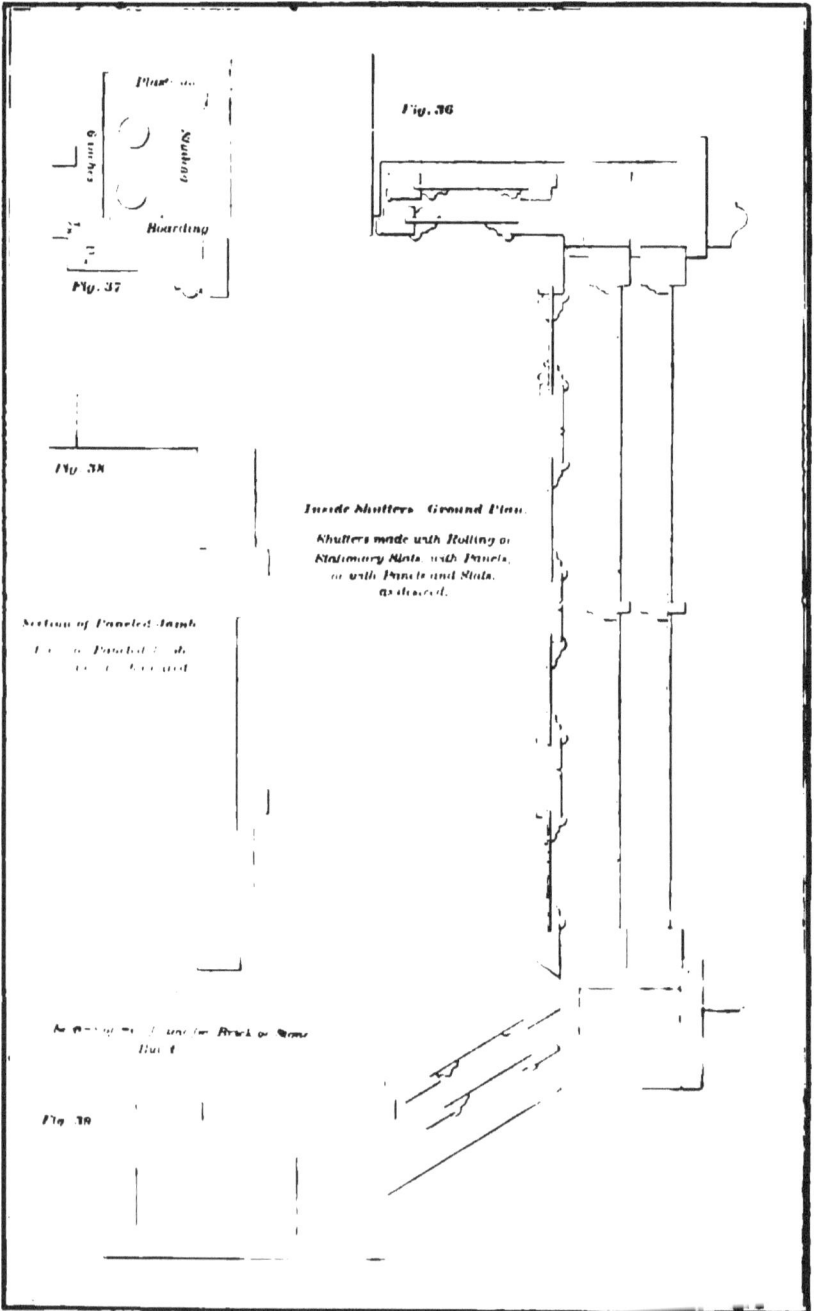

Fig. 36

Plate

Bolting

Boarding

Fig. 37

Fig. 38

Inside Shutters Ground Plan.

Shutters made with Rolling or
Stationary Slats, with Panels,
or with Panels and Slats,
as desired.

Section of Paneled Jamb

Fig. 39

GEORGE J. GRIFFIN,

ENGLISH, FRENCH,

GERMAN & AMERICAN SEEDS

Dutch Flowering Bulbs, &c.

AGRICULTURAL SEED DEPARTMENT

VEGETABLE SEED DEPARTMENT

FLOWER SEED DEPARTMENT

GEORGE J GRIFFIN

GEORGE ELMS & SONS,

CONTRACTORS,

CARPENTERS & JOINERS,

RICHMOND STREET NORTH,

(Between John and Mill Streets.)

ALL ORDERS PROMPTLY ATTENDED TO.

JOHN FERGUSON,

Upholsterer and Undertaker,

KING STREET,

Second Door from Revere House,

LONDON, - ONTARIO.